ROYAL BODIES

Royal Bodies

Writing about the Windsors from

the *London Review of Books*

London Review of Books
28 Little Russell Street, London WC1A 2HN

ISBN 978 1 9996361 0 4

Typeset by LRB (London) Limited
The text is set in FF Quadraat

Series editor: Sam Kinchin-Smith
Cover illustration: Anne Rothenstein
Cover design: Kit Humphrey

Printed and bound in Great Britain by Clays Ltd St Ives

lrb.co.uk

Contents

Introduction

Thomas Jones

'PEOPLE SOMETIMES ASK ME why I moan on so much about the royal family,' Glen Newey wrote on the LRB blog in 2013. 'Aren't there more important things to worry about, like war, political repression, man-made climate change or Arsenal's exit from the Champions League? To give the short answer, yes. But in a funny way, no.' He was writing about a 'kerosene-guzzling beano to the Middle East' that Prince Charles had gone on, and the ways in which the activities of the royals can contribute to important things like war, political repression and man-made climate change, as well as the way 'they exemplify hierarchy and hereditary privilege.'

Still, as the pieces in this selection make clear, the *London Review* hasn't taken a clear editorial stance on the monarchy over the last forty years.* In 1995, Alan Bennett wrote about turning his play *The Madness of George III* into a movie. 'I'm no republican,' he said in passing; the words made their way onto the cover of the paper. In 2007 we ran Bennett's story 'The Uncommon Reader' – too long, regrettably, to include in an anthology – in which the queen, or an affectionately imagined version of her, discovers a belated love of reading. And in 1987, in the first of the pieces

---

* Our editorial stance on capitalisation has changed, too; around ten years ago we stopped saying 'the Queen' and started saying 'the queen' instead (taking all her relatives down with her). In this volume the minusculisation occurs between Jenny Diski's piece on Diana and Bee Wilson's on Edward VII.

collected here, we published a memoir by William Empson, written in 1955, about the masque he had written for the queen when she visited Sheffield University the year before. 'It is, I believe, the first time English royalty has been given the real old flattery for three hundred years,' he later told his publisher, arguing for the masque's inclusion in his *Collected Poems*. 'It isn't meant to be good poetry but it's somehow politically right (I mean, it combines queen-worship with pro-worker sentiment and fair claims for the university back-room boys).'

Empson found the queen both 'personally charming' and 'sensible'. Her sister's charm was of a different kind entirely. Princess Margaret, Ferdinand Mount writes, was not only 'ghastly' but 'ghastly in a way that brings out the worst in other people'. One of the reasons for her ghastliness may have been that she wasn't allowed to marry Peter Townsend. 'It soured her for good,' Mount says. 'It was a backhanded mercy that she did not live to hear the bells ringing to celebrate the engagement of Prince Harry to a divorced American actor of mixed race,' Mount concludes. 'Wallis Simpson, too, must be turning in her unquiet grave.'

According to Paul Foot's review of Charles Haigh's 1988 biography of Simpson, the reason Edward VIII was forced to abdicate had less to do with his lover's nationality or marital status than with her politics. 'For all its weaknesses,' Foot writes, 'the book is enthralling from first to last and for one central reason. It exposes both its main subject and her royal catch, not as the dim-witted, self-obsessed lovers who have been pickled for posterity, but as nasty, determined Fascists.' Diana Mosley wrote to the paper to deny that she and her husband had dined with the Windsors twice a week.

We seem to have published at least as many pieces on those who married into the royal family as on those who were born into it (and, in Princess Margaret's case, prevented from marrying out of it). 'It isn't entirely obvious,' Jenny Diski wrote in

2007, ten years after Princess Diana died, 'what fascinated people so about ... the uneducated, O-level-free daughter of an ancient house, former nanny, Sloane, clothes-horse, playgirl, campaigner, therapist addict.' Lack of O-levels is a theme: Camilla Shand, as she then was, went to finishing school in Switzerland 'armed with only one O-level', Caroline Murphy writes; Mount reminds us that Princess Margaret never went to school. Though in some ways that may have been preferable to the education the future Edward VII received from his parents, which was, Bee Wilson writes, 'monstrously harsh', and 'neither reined him in nor sharpened him up'.

Diana's death looked for a while as if it might spell the final collapse of the monarchy, already tottering since the failure of the marriages of most of the queen's children. Earlier in 1997, Tom Nairn wrote that 'all that the Crown now accomplishes is to counterpoint and somehow exaggerate an ambient unreality: the new, motherless country left behind by its moral decease.' Who could have predicted two decades ago that Camilla Parker Bowles, as she then was, would walk up at the aisle at Prince William's wedding in 2011 as the Duchess of Cornwall, a few steps ahead of the queen? (Scandals pass and fade: in a 2003 piece on the memoirs of Paul Burrell – Diana's butler – I mentioned a 'monarchy-obliterating secret that lurks on Fleet St'; I now have no clue what I was referring to.)

Hilary Mantel's piece on 'royal bodies' was published 18 months after William and Kate's wedding. It's partly about the Duchess of Cambridge, then pregnant with her first child, though it's also about Diana, Marie Antoinette and Anne Boleyn, and the ways in which women's bodies have been instrumentalised (not that Mantel uses the word) by the monarchy and its observers. The piece was seized on by the press, the *Daily Mail* as ever at the head of the pack, slathering with righteous indignation at what it called a 'venomous attack' on the duchess. Mantel patiently explained that the passages the *Mail* et al. objected to were 'describing the perception of her which has been set up in the tabloid press'. Which may explain the real reason for their outrage.

Newey's disrespectful piece on the royal family's 'latest annus horribilis', which appeared in January 2003, was overlooked by the *Mail*. But a subscriber came to the office to express in person his displeasure at our having published it. He was almost speechless with rage at the coarseness of the piece. Did we realise that his wife read the paper? (No mention of his servants.) This book is not for him.

Other unhappy readers feel that we have the opposite problem: not a lack of deference to the Windsors, but a surfeit of it. Earlier this year we received a long complaint from a subscriber in Canada. Among other things, a 'review of the *LRB*'s calibre publishing rubbish piece after rubbish [piece] on the monarchy,' he wrote, 'is becoming tedious.' This book is not for him, either.

The Queen and I

William Empson

I SUPPOSE I HAVE NO BUSINESS to print any remarks made in comparative private by the Queen of England, or indeed by the Vice-Chancellor of Sheffield University: but as what I have to say is solely to their credit I do not expect it to annoy anyone. Indeed, you might feel that these remarks are merely a piece of boasting, and have the inherent dullness of that process: but I should expect a reader to feel, as I did, that the whole affair was anxious somehow. It was a matter of reviving the real old half-blasphemous flattery of the Renaissance which I don't suppose has been proffered to any English royalty for three hundred years. One was bound to be rather doubtful about how it would go off.

The Queen was touring the industrial areas of the North of England, at her usual gruelling speed; Sheffield has long been a big steel town; and it was somehow protocol while she was there for her to include the University, because of a fifty-year anniversary since its royal foundation. The Vice-Chancellor decided it would be a good thing to have a masque, chiefly to recall the way the first Queen Elizabeth was habitually received on similar tours: he set up a committee to agree on the plot and production of this, and asked me to do the writing (which of course entranced me), adding a caveat that he wanted no fuss about archaic language or style. He offered a specimen draft of a plot himself, and I wish I could remember how much of the final version he had already invented. He was clear anyhow that the thing would be pointless if not all

[5]

about making steel. He suggested, I remember, the display of a figure in full Vice-Chancellor's robes first jeered at and then turned
by a goddess into a real steel technician. He himself is a scientist
who, as so often, is fretted by being turned into an administrator,
so that the sentiment was known by the committee to be a genuine
one: but we felt it was only meant to set the right tone. It was I,
as I remember, who insisted that the goddess must descend from
Heaven in a 'car', because that used to be the regular thing – not
foreseeing what an enormous amount of architecture this would
finally involve. In any case, I hope it is clear that I was called in as
one of the technicians; it did not cross any of our minds that the
'style' of the poet Empson was wanted; what the writing had to do
was to put across the old savage fantastic thing very shortly and
clearly. On the other hand, you did need to be careful about your
politics; I remember being very worried, later on in committee, at
one of the changes required by the producer, until we thought of a
new verse line which got our political face straight again. Clearly,
it is not enough merely to worship the Queen by telling her to her
face that she is the universal spirit who creates everything, nor indeed (to take the other view of the affair) is it enough just to make
the steel industry look ridiculous so as to amuse the Queen, only
for a moment, after she has had her nose rubbed in it very heavily and before she has her tea. Perhaps I should remark that many
people in England realise that we live on food from abroad, and
would actually stop eating if the steel industry went wrong. What
you had got to do (even though at your great expense you were only
aiming at a very light little bit of spoof) was to be fair enough to
the Trades Unions and the Managements and the Back-Room-Boy
specialists in the university itself, or anyhow not to sound like bad
feeling to any of them. If the whole thing is a joke, and the jokes
keep on being altered for technical reasons, it takes a lot of watching to make sure that one of them doesn't slide sideways.

May I also remark that, as a literary critic, I can claim the dismal eminence of being the only expert on the subject of 'A is B' (see *The Structure of Complex Words*), so that being actually set to tell the Queen that she is a Goddess appeared to me a fascinating field of study. I am not sure that the Vice-Chancellor realised what strong forces were coming up: I suspect he first thought it would be nice to do a graceful little bit of historical reminiscence, but before you knew where you were it was really happening.

About a hundred years ago, as I understand, when Queen Victoria went into retirement as a widow, the English very nearly got rid of the Crown; there was practically nobody in favour of it. They began to get fond of it when she appeared again being noticeably old, and since then it has gone steadily up and up. But you wouldn't have revived the worship of the first Elizabeth for any of them before the second Elizabeth. However, this is not to say that the students were keen to come and do the heavy amount of work involved; I gather there was an almost alarming amount of difficulty about raising the very large requirement of supers for incessant rehearsal. One evening I went to a rehearsal which seemed to me particularly dismal, and I did what I would not have done if I had not been a little tipsy (merely more noisy and friendly than usual). When the producer said they could go and have coffee I beat on the table and said, 'No, I wish first to address the entire cast' – perhaps two hundred persons, all gloomy, you understand. I told them that they must not think this just tiresomely absurd, they must realise that it was wildly strange: nobody had told royalty it was a divine creative spirit for three hundred years, and the whole lay-out of this ad-hoc theatre, with the Queen in a high glass cage before them, addressed personally, and any other audience only let creep in along the sides, made it the strangest performance they were ever going to take part in. The mad king of Bavaria could not get what they were getting. And so I went on. I next found myself in the gentlemen's lavatory, alongside a severe character who I imagine to have been an electrician, and I asked rather anxiously what he thought about my speech. His answer was surprisingly warm, but from my point of view quite off the point. 'It was plumb right,' he said, 'you got just the right timing. There's just a week to go, and they'll be all right once they feel in the straight' – a metaphor from horse racing – 'but what they feel now is that they can't bear any more rehearsing.' The interest of this kind of thing, to me, if I may patiently explain, was that you could not get anybody to take the faintest interest in the historical revival of the Renaissance half-worship of the first Elizabeth: in one way they weren't bothered with any idea that you could treat the thing seriously, in another way they felt it was the only adequate reception for the present Queen.

The music composed for the occasion, as I found when I got back from a trip to America, had turned out staggeringly magnificent; and I began to be afraid that the audience would be disgusted and would think the flattery of the Queen 'fulsome'. Someone had cut out a tiny joke, which was felt to get in the way of the grandeur of the music: there I had to make another solemn harangue, this time to a large committee, fighting to get back my little joke, or whatever you might call it – it is more like a sergeant-major barking out at the audience: 'laugh.' I was allowed this paltry little thing back, and it did make the only laugh in the show. The point of this anecdote, may I tiresomely explain, is that the whole thing had become alarmingly more serious than we had originally expected.

Perhaps I should quote. It is just after Minerva has descended in her car, and her first words were to be:

Majesty, I am yourself. As you would wish
I now create SHEFFIELD. This poor fish

(presenting laboratory overalls to the Alchemist, who immediately dons them)

I turn into a steel technician;
And every worker to a real magician

(rehabilitation somehow of entire chorus). The producer, who brilliantly made a solid body out of the skeleton I offered, broke these couplets at the word 'Sheffield' and gave the goddess three new couplets, so that she could turn three serfs into three types of skilled worker, with a lot of business and music, and then they agreed to throw away the rhyme 'fish'.

By the time the music has been copied out (with words and exact timing) for the enormous orchestra there is no question of altering this arrangement. But, as I claimed, there is an obvious difference in whether the Goddess is talking to the serfs on the stage or to the real Queen. She has only to step forward and resume her personal address to the Queen, on the words 'This poor fish', and will then, after the strain of this long pause, satisfy the audience by completing her first rhyming couplet. This she absolutely must do, because a pantomime fairy queen *always* talks in bad rhyming couplets, and always has done since the time of Shakespeare. The difficulty was to get it into the head of the student actress, whose natural dignity was otherwise splendid for the part, that she really must look at the Queen and address her unofficially and as if otherwise unheard – they are secretly plotting together. She said it was impossible (she had also to keep in time to background music), but I think she did it all right on the day. Anyhow, I won back that silly 'fish', and whether anybody in the audience realised it was a bad rhyme or not it did get the only laugh in the whole show. What I said in my harangue was, 'You don't realise – this will become intolerable unless you force a laugh into it early enough', and when we had our delighted boasting-party after the show my opponents handsomely agreed I had been right.

I pass now to the reactions of the Queen, who was so generous to everybody concerned and so determined to be as much in public as possible that it seems correct to report her. The mechanics of our being presented to her had to be a bit out of shape; lots of people were going to be presented to her. I was told to come down and talk to her in the crowded room (such was the elaborate planning of the few minutes), until the producer and the composer and the two speaking actors could get round from the stage, so I rather unfairly had the first reactions alone. Late in the boasting-party the producer formed a dark suspicion, and said to me rather crossly: 'Professor Empson, had you *really* never met the Queen before?' When I die, I shall still think that the most exquisite flattery I have ever received. It seems to be regular that you are first filtered through the Duke of Edinburgh, who seriously (and plausibly) thinks that the Queen might work herself to death if he wasn't there to stop it. I naturally had my piece to say to him about the masques done for the first Queen Elizabeth when on tour, and he caught me up sharp when I said they wouldn't have given her dancing because they couldn't do it. He says: 'Of course they could.' Empson says: 'Yes, of course they had their own dancing, but they couldn't do *court* dancing, the *court* masque is an entirely different thing, with no audience at all really, because the Queen herself would often dance. But when on tour the first Elizabeth would always be received with a bit of music and a bit of poetry, just like we have here.' This seemed enough to handle it, and then he said (of course he is very much an English military officer, a type of man who is very much pleasanter to deal with than the English legend pretends) that he thought it was a good plan to have this sort of show, because it gave a lot of them something to do, and they would always rather have something to do, really. 'Yes,' I said, lying, and I crawled across and told this story exactly as if it was my own straight back to the Queen, because I had been briefed. I shall always think this rather a mean action, because the truth was that it had become rather rough to get enough students to perform in this thing. But I shall always be far more thankful that I wasn't fool enough to tell a tiny nasty truth to the Queen. The first fact about the Queen is that she is magical, because she is a charming woman who actually has by law the peculiar position which every charming woman feels she ought to have. At this point she had to wait and let me talk, with about two hundred people waiting to be presented, because it had been agreed that the subject of the play had better be finished off first. I thus found myself in the position of being required to hold the staggering royalty in conversation, before a large audience of my resentful colleagues, for an indefinite length of time. It was extremely short.

This has happened to me before, about 1932 in Japan, in the Japan-British Society, to which Prince Chichibu (younger brother of Emperor Hirohito) liked to come (he had been educated in England and was at that time heir to the throne). I went there after a bit of grumbling at the expense, because, though a professor is practically invisible, I didn't want to be out of any fun. A British minor diplomat yanked me by the collar and said, 'You talk to Chichibu' – because a diplomat could only address him in the very peculiar Japanese used only to royalty, where I would without breaking protocol address him in English, which of course he knew perfectly. It is like suddenly finding yourself on a lighted stage without knowing your lines. I shall always think better of myself because I thought at once of a tolerable thing to say to this friendly character. I said, 'Why don't you start a pack of hounds here in Japan?' and these were the only words I needed to say. Chichibu immediately said that there was a fortune waiting for the first man who would start a pack of hounds in Japan, but the master would have to work in with the very peculiar fox-superstitions of the peasants. He must be both a fox god himself and a saviour of the fox god, but it wasn't hard to do, and Chichibu was going into great detail about this when suddenly I was yanked from the collar because a British diplomat had arrived who was prepared to address Chichibu in the very peculiar Japanese used only to royalty. Considering that after my first sentence I had expressed nothing except cries of pleasure, I hope I do not appear vain in reporting that I thought this interruption must have appeared tiresome to Chichibu: after all, he could not possibly have come to this peculiar club unless he had wanted to behave like he was doing to me. This incident was my only previous contact with royalty, and it left stuck in my head that royalty wants to be addressed in an unfrightened manner, so long as the manner is not impudent or politically wrong.

I am deliberately sporting with the impatience of my reader, and he or she has worse to come. I have made a serious rule in my life *never* to take part in post-mortems over a party or write nasty books about what my kind hosts said to me in any part of the world; and, as I found myself having to say very soon after this incident, I literally do not know what was said. However, I am afraid I do know what really happened. I lectured the Queen (please remember it was protocol – I had been told to hold her in conversation) and as always when lecturing I shut my eyes. This is a very stupid thing to do when talking to the Queen, because her face ought to be watched incessantly. All the same, a flat lecture about the behaviour of the first Elizabeth could not appear off the point.

We at Sheffield wondered whether to do a dance masque, I was telling her, but I am glad we didn't because it would have been historically unlike what the first Elizabeth would have seen on tour. The Devil here (in the masque) is a fully-trained ballet dancer, and she has made the entire cast do fantastic physical-training exercises before every performance. But it would be historically wrong to make a court masque of it. Consider, I said, opening my eyes and at last looking at her, after talking much longer than this account, that in a real court masque the Queen herself danced. She met the eyes, and the subject dropped. I am not only a bad reporter, I have positively taught myself to be a bad reporter, so I do not know at what point the Queen (who of course had simply taken into her head that she was in favour of this entertainment, and wasn't surprised that the various characters concerned with it seemed a bit rough when presented) said to me that she liked the play because it was so light. The possibility of saying, 'Come, come, mam, what degree of blasphemous flattery *would* you call heavy?' not only could not but did not attract the mind of Empson. What the Queen said was not only true but sensible. I said: 'Well, it was meant to be funny, but the way it turned out, we only got one laugh in the whole show.' She said – and unless you consider the extraordinary architecture of this performance run up for the Queen alone, you do not realise the startling effect of this sane reply: 'Yes, I was very interested in that too, I was watching the audience with great interest. I *thought* that the reason why they didn't laugh at the jokes was that they had all heard them several times before.' 'Yes, mam, quite right,' I said, lying again; if I had thought to discuss that, the thing would have been too long altogether.

You must remember that the actual capacities of the Queen really appear above human; the wildly strange facts about her begin to cross the mind of a man who considers her behaviour. From what I gather, she can take on two hundred presentations within ten minutes, finishing on the dot, and every man jack feels he has been spoken to personally. A certain reverence is always felt towards a race-horse, because it is such a staggeringly delicate and highly-trained animal, and it is wonderful to stumble by accident in walking across country upon one of the secret paddocks deeply curtained by trees where these animals are growing up in seclusion. Now if you take breeding seriously, as a farmer has to do, you want all the mothers as well, and the only conclusion you could get to in the case of the Queen is that she comes from healthy stock; it is a mere delusion to think that she has been inbred like a race-horse. But such is the basic fact, felt by anybody who comes near the Queen – that what you are really dealing with is not as you might think a charming woman but a slightly legendary animal, like a race-horse, for instance. You had better be very careful about it.

I could not conceivably have enough time to discuss the matter. What had happened was that the old worship of Kings (it isn't so old – it is just a result of breaking with the Pope in Europe, though of course among savages it is ancestral) had really been felt again. It is already felt about Elizabeth, whose personal charm I have not yet had occasion to mention: but it did occur to me, while I was allowed to yatter to her merely to wait for the cast of the play to turn up, in front of the mob of two hundred or so who were waiting to be presented to her, that the joke had become true. This is a rather unnerving position for an imaginative writer, as Paul Goodman very well and rather thrillingly insisted when he said: 'Suppose the two things happen together; suppose the deep ancestral unconsciousness which the man has fully and successfully repressed is merely the same as what his society asks him to do. This is not only probable, it happens nearly all the time. Doesn't he feel pleased?' I greatly respect the good sense of this remark, but the pleasure I want to boast about is a rather unusual one. When Minerva turned up in her full warpaint to meet the Queen at tea (please remember that the whole purpose of the play was to say that she is identical with the Queen), I cried out with a natural ironical rich friendly pleasure, 'Now, at last, they meet,' and the Queen said: 'I envied you your ride in the car.' She could not have answered better after a week of Sundays with ten committees. It was so gracious that it came pretty near accepting a legend. Now, in the old days (very recent) when it was the custom to do this kind of flattery to royalty, other persons were extremely noisy all the time about what a wicked thing it is to do to royalty, because it goes to their heads, as anybody can see, and makes them behave badly. Do you know, I was so genuinely 16th-century that I became anxious not to turn Elizabeth's head, when I found everybody around madly determined to turn Elizabeth's head. As so often, my anxieties were ridiculous, but they were in the right direction. Elizabeth would have had a kick like a mule if she had thought anything wrong, but, after she had watched the audience carefully throughout the performance (and the architecture had been addressed so singly to herself that it was actually physically hard for her to realise that there were any other spectators), she had decided that the thing had been in bad taste.

The point of this story is that I was downright thrilled to hear the Queen herself show that she wasn't a lunatic. I want to put it in the flattest possible language, because we ought never to forget that this worship of royalty has in the past taken very bad forms: but what she really did was to show that she saw all round the question. What the well-meaning (and in the event very right) Vice-Chancellor had asked me to do was not merely a short old-world reminiscence for the University but a raising of deep sentiment which involved a very serious test of the sanity of the Queen. Her husband and her mother would agree at once that this kind of thing would have to be stopped if it was going to her head. But, as it couldn't conceivably go to her head, as she would automatically be watching the audience with great interest, whatever the performance was, I need not have puzzled you about this legally conceivable difficulty. But there it is: you can't have a man doing this kind of work unless he is imagining for himself the various kinds of difficulty that might possibly crop up.

I have not yet mentioned the decisive fact, what I am really talking about, though you will think it a bore when it comes: it is the charm of the Queen. Well now, to start with, you can't laugh it off. We have a very good American staying with us here this year, and he will not grudge my reporting that after sitting among six random English teachers at lunch in the teachers' club, with every one of them praising the charm of the Queen, he was at last stung into telling stories which proved the decisive and thrilling charm of General Eisenhower. This was considered a joke, in its way, among plenty of other jokes about royalty: but he was telling something true there. They both have wide mouths. I have told my little boys that if they want to become kings they have only to put their two thumbs in their mouths every night and rip their cheeks apart. An enormous mouth is essential to modern royalty. You are probably thinking back on me, that I can only talk in this easy way because my whole upbringing makes me feel good enough class to speak to the Queen, so it is only a typical English boast. You are quite right, and what is more I had quite enough to say to the Queen during the very brief time when I was required by protocol to speak to her, so when I confess I ended by feeling downright awe, without having been snubbed for a moment but only treated with a kind of determined kindness till the other characters from the play arrived, it is perhaps plausible to report that the Queen was quite enough to handle Empson. I did not see her beauty till the other characters arrived, so I felt comparatively at leisure. It is an astonishingly mobile performance when the Queen wishes to congratulate – not only the incredibly wide movement of the mouth. I had seen her just before the show reading an official statement of approval to Sheffield University, for which we were all grandly dressed, and my heart sank to my boots because she looked as cross as a camel, and maybe you don't know how cross a camel looks, but if she felt like that our little bit of fun was going to be quite hopeless. When she came back from the 13 minutes of this enormously planned performance in her honour, and could at last sit down to her cup of tea, her face was not so much changed as mobile again and prepared to go through all its changes. I was kindly spoken to by one of the secretaries of the Queen, after my performance was over, and he naturally spoke of her with the reverence, and the anxiety for her health, that a man feels for his own peculiar performing animal. It was hard for her to have to read that speech, he said, but now of course it's all right. 'Now' was just when she was giving just enough praise to each one of two hundred men, each of whom would go home and boast of it for the rest of their lives. It struck me at once, as I said to him, that this must be a different kind of animal to me. I could read out any speech without bothering, if it was short enough to look over during a few minutes in the lavatory: but if ever I tried to do what she's doing now, while you say she's feeling comfortable, it would put me straight into a lunatic asylum.

I ought to have said before that Mr Kennedy, the composer of the masque, got on very well with the Duke of Edinburgh, because the composer is really an expert on cancer, and so is the Duke, and so all this elaborately staged scene could thankfully be let drop while they talked quite seriously. At any moment, it always struck me, you might get this startling drop onto the facts of life, but when you did drop it was always onto a solid pavement. All the same, the persons concerned could not have built up this eerie note of fantasy about the whole affair unless they could feel certain beforehand that they were dealing with a Queen who was not only personally charming enough to carry it off but also sensible enough.

26 November 1987

The great times
they could have had

Paul Foot

A GREAT MANY BOOKS and articles have been published recently about the possibility that a former head of MI5 was the agent of a foreign power. Could there be anything more horrible, more unthinkable? Well, yes, according to Charles Higham's extraordinary biography, there could.* He suggests that not long ago the most dangerous agent of a foreign power was the King; and the second most dangerous was the King's lover. Both were sympathetic to, and possibly active agents for, Mussolini and Hitler at a time when the British Government was about to declare war on Italy and Germany.

Mr Higham's book has been greeted with a tremendous shout of fury. 'Universally slated' was how Sidgwick and Jackson described its reception to me. It has been passed over for serialisation. Film rights, once assured, are now in jeopardy. Writing in the *Spectator*, Frances Donaldson, modestly omitting to refer to her own worthy, if rather pedestrian biography of Edward VIII, could not contain her indignation. 'Nor am I alone in thinking it rather shocking,' she boomed, 'that Mr Higham was able to find a reputable British publisher for his book.'

Lady Donaldson doesn't believe for a moment that either the Duke or Duchess of Windsor were even pro-Nazi. She follows in

---

* *Wallis: Secret Lives of the Duchess of Windsor* (Sidgwick, 1988).

a long line of biographers, historians and journalists who concede, since it is plainly on the record, that the Duke and Duchess were both opposed to war with Germany, but who dismiss the idea that they were sympathetic to Fascism as a 'mistaken notion' (Brian Inglis's conclusion in his 1966 account, *Abdication*). Lady Donaldson denounces Charles Higham for retailing tittle-tattle, and concludes that if you leave out the gossip and the speculation there is nothing left in his biography which we didn't know before.

What is the picture so gaudily painted by Mr Higham? Wallis Warfield was born (out of wedlock) into a rich and comfortable middle-class family in Baltimore. She went to high-society schools, where she read Kipling to her boyfriends. She married a young Air Force officer, and became, in her twenties, an important personality in Washington society. Her main male friend outside her collapsing marriage was the Ambassador in Washington of the new Fascist regime in Italy, Prince Gelasio Caetani, an attractive and powerful propagandist for Mussolini. While still friendly with Caetani, Wallis forged even closer bonds with Felipe Espil, First Secretary at the Argentinian Embassy in Washington, an ardent Fascist and a representative of the savage Irigoyen dictatorship in Buenos Aires.

Mr Higham, who has certainly done his homework in the American state files, produces clear evidence that Wallis Spencer, as she then was, was hired as an agent for Naval Intelligence. The purpose of her visit to China in the mid-Twenties, where she accompanied her husband, who also worked for Intelligence, was to carry secret papers between the American Government and the warlords they supported against the Communists. In Peking her consort for a time was Alberto de Zara, Naval Attaché at the Italian Embassy, whose enthusiasm for Mussolini was often expressed in verse. When she moved to Shanghai, she made another close friend in another dashing young Fascist, Count

Galeazzo Ciano, later Mussolini's Foreign Secretary. Wallis's enthusiasm for the Italian dictatorship was, by this time, the only thing she had in common with her husband, Winfield Spencer. In 1936, ten years after the couple were divorced, Spencer was awarded the Order of the Crown of Italy, one of the highest decorations of the Mussolini regime.

Ernest Simpson, the dull partner in a shipping firm whom Wallis married in 1928, had close business ties with Fascist Italy. But her feeling for Fascism cannot be attributed only to her men friends. On the contrary, the 'new social order' brayed around the world by the Italian dictator and his representatives fitted precisely with Wallis's own upbringing, character and disposition. She was all her life an intensely greedy woman, obsessed with her own property and how she could make more of it. She was a racist through and through: anti-semitic, except when she hoped to benefit from rich Jewish friends; and anti-black ('Government House with only a coloured staff would put me in my grave,' she moaned when, many years later, her husband was the Governor of the Bahamas). She was offensive to her servants, and hated the class they came from.

Her Fascist sympathies stayed with her all her life. When she needed a lawyer to start a libel action in 1937, she chose the Parisian Nazi Armand Grégoire. Even when the war was on, she fraternised with the pro-Nazi French businessman, Charles Bedaux. Perhaps her most consistent British confidante and friend was Diana Mosley, Sir Oswald's wife. As the Windsors and the Mosleys grew old in exile, they took regular solace together, meeting and dining twice a week and musing about the great times they could have had if only the British had seen sense and sided with Hitler and Mussolini against the Reds.

Of all the bonds which united this dreadful woman to the glamorous Prince of Wales in the late-Twenties, none was so strong as their shared politics. Charles Higham's biography sets out the facts about the Prince's Fascist leanings and sympathy with the Nazi cause and the corporate state in Italy. The Prince was proud of his German origins, spoke German fluently, and felt an emotional, racial and intellectual solidarity with the Nazi leaders. As early as July 1933, with Hitler only just ensconced as German Chancellor, Robert Bruce-Lockhart records conversations between the Prince and the grandson of the former Kaiser, Prince Louis-Ferdinand: 'The Prince of Wales was quite pro-Hitler and said it was no business of ours to interfere in Germany's internal affairs either re Jews or anything else, and added that the dictators are very popular these days, and that we might want one in England before long.' Not long afterwards the Prince confided in a former Austrian ambassador, Count Mensdorff, who wrote: 'It is remarkable how he expressed his sympathies for the Nazis ...'

Such sympathies were of course common, at least for a while, in London society, but when others began to waver, the Prince of Wales remained steadfast. He asked the Germans to fix up a special dinner for him at the German Embassy, as a special mark of his solidarity with their government. The Germans, on instructions from Berlin, invited Mrs Simpson, who was then his paramour. The company he kept in London burgeoned with keen young supporters of the Nazi 'experiment'. Edward ('Fruity') Metcalfe, one of his closest friends, and the best man at his wedding to Wallis, appeared in the *Tatler* dressed up in Fascist regalia at a 'Blackshirt' dinner. When the Foreign Secretary Samuel Hoare fixed up a deal with Pierre Laval, the French Foreign Secretary and a Nazi fellow-traveller, to legitimise Mussolini's conquest of Abyssinia, the Duke also travelled to France. Whatever part he played in the Hoare-Laval Pact, he enthusiastically supported it when it was completed.

In all the innumerable versions of the 'Greatest Love Story of the Century' it is assumed that the British Establishment, led by Stanley Baldwin and the Archbishop of Canterbury, could not stomach the idea of a monarch marrying a twice-divorced woman. The objections, it is said, were moral and religious. The truth is, however, that throughout the centuries archbishops and prime ministers have miraculously overcome their moral objections to royal idiosyncrasies in the bedchamber. The real objection to the liaison between the King and Mrs Simpson was that both were Nazi sympathisers at a time when the more far-sighted civil servants, politicians and businessmen were beginning, sometimes reluctantly, to realise that British interests and German interests were on a collision course. As the biographers of Baldwin, Keith Middlemas and John Barnes, observed, 'the government had awakened to a danger that had nothing to do with any question of marriage.'

Charles Higham quotes an FBI file in Washington: 'Certain would-be state secrets were passed on to Edward, and when it was found that Ribbentrop' – the German Ambassador in London – 'actually received the same information, immediately Baldwin was forced to accept that the leakage had been located.' Higham then asserts (without quoting the relevant passage): 'The same report categorically states that Wallis was responsible for this breach of security.' Of Sir Robert Vansittart, Permanent Under-Secretary at the Foreign Office and head of British Intelligence, Higham writes (and here he does provide the evidence): he 'was Wallis's implacable enemy from the day he was convinced she was a Nazi collaborator'.

It is this, far more than any moral consideration, which explains the determination and the ruthlessness with which Baldwin and his administration dealt with the King before his abdication. They were prepared to put up with him, as long as he was acting on his own. They bypassed him. By midsummer 1936, Higham writes, 'all confidential documents were withheld from the King.' The prospect of a Nazi King backed up by an infinitely more able and resourceful Wallis Simpson was intolerable. If the

King wanted Mrs Simpson, he would have to get out. If he wanted to stay as King, she would have to be banished. The King's
choice (the 'woman I love', and exile) came as a great relief to the
Government. Yet Edward remained a menace as he continued,
in his exile, to offer the Nazis solidarity. When war broke out, he
was summoned back to England and sent to France on military
duty with the rank of Major-General. His lack of interest and enthusiasm for the job, which he showed by coolly abandoning his
duties to attend some parties in the South of France with Wallis,
would, in normal circumstances, have led to a court-martial. The
Duke of Windsor was not court-martialled. He was made Governor of the Bahamas.

Wherever he went, people noted his Nazi sympathies, which
were fanned to fury by the Duchess. As early as 1937, Sir Ronald
Lindsay, British Ambassador to Washington, wrote to his wife
that the Duke of Windsor was 'trying to stage a comeback, and
his friends and advisers were semi-Nazis'. A month or two later,
Lindsay wrote, officially: 'The active supporters of the Duke of
Windsor within England are those elements known to have in-
clinations towards Fascist dictatorships, and the recent tour of
Germany by the Duke of Windsor and his ostentatious reception
by Hitler and his regime can only be construed as a willingness
on the part of the Duke of Windsor to lend himself to these ten-
dencies.' On that tour, the Duke seemed to take special pleasure
in greeting the enthusiastic crowds with the Nazi salute. Years
afterwards, he would proudly show his guests the pictures of
him and Wallis being greeted by the Führer. David Eccles, then
a young civil servant, met the Duke and Duchess in Spain and
reported 'The Duke is pretty fifth column.' In Portugal, the
German Ambassador, Oswald Baron von Hoyningen-Heune,
relayed to his superiors in Berlin the Duke's conviction that
'had he remained on the throne, war could have been avoided.'
'He describes himself,' von Hoyningen-Heune continued, 'as a

firm supporter of a compromise peace with Germany. The Duke believes with certainty that continued heavy bombing will make England ready for peace.'

Many opponents of the view that the Duke and Duchess were active supporters of the Nazis throughout these times point to his interest in workers' conditions and to his visit to South Wales in 1936, when he made the famous (and fatuous) statement that 'something should be done' about unemployment. Yet the provision of good facilities for hardworking people was crucial to the Nazi idea of a 'new social order' and a key to its popularity.

Once they were exiled to the Bahamas, and closely watched by both British and American Intelligence, the royal couple's Nazi sympathies were kept in check. Even there, however, they associated with Fascist businessmen, in particular the corrupt Harold Christie, with whom the Duke, with the help of the Bahamian taxpayer, went into partnership. As the war swung towards the Allies, the couple's enthusiasm for the Nazis began to lose its fervour, and in their autobiographies, written much later, both Duke and Duchess would take refuge in the familiar excuse that they had underestimated the horror of the Fascist regimes.

Their former adversaries in the British Government and Civil Service were among the many people who assisted them in their rewriting of their past. The Duke's brother, George VI, made every effort to ensure that the fact that the King of England had been a Hitler supporter before the war was kept under wraps. Armand Grégoire, the Duchess's Nazi lawyer, was tried for collusion with the enemy and sent to prison for life, without being asked for (or volunteering) information about his role as intermediary between the royal couple and his Nazi masters. Charles Bedaux, who might have been persuaded to trade some such information in exchange for lenient treatment, committed suicide while under arrest for treason. Coco Chanel, an intimate friend of the Duchess, was arrested and charged with treason against the French state. The evidence against her was prodigious. She had worked directly for Nazi Intelligence against her own government. After a 24-hour interrogation by American Intelligence, however, she was released. 'Had she been forced to stand trial, with the threat of execution as an employee of an enemy government,' Higham writes, 'she could easily have exposed as Nazi collaborators the Windsors and dozens of others highly placed in society. Despite the hatred of the Windsors at Buckingham Palace, the royal family would not willingly tolerate an exposé of a member of the family.'

This sense of solidarity prompted the King to send the Keeper of the Royal Pictures on a secret mission to Germany soon after the war to collect from the Schloss Kronberg, family home of the Princes of Hesse, a bundle of documents which exposed the connection between the Windsors and the Nazis. The Keeper of the Royal Pictures and an associate went to great lengths to retrieve these papers, which have never been seen since. The Keeper of the Royal Pictures was Anthony Blunt, who for nearly ten years had been an active agent of the Russian Government. By 1945 Blunt's loyalty to his king had superseded his loyalty to Communism, and he kept quiet about his secret mission. In 1964, when he finally confessed to his KGB past, his interrogator was a middle-ranking MI5 man called Peter Wright. Wright was summoned to the Palace. On the one hand, he was told by Michael Adeane, the Queen's private secretary, that the Palace would do all they could to help, and, on the other, warned that Blunt might mention his trip to Germany after the war, and ordered abruptly not to pursue this particular matter. In the event, despite hundreds of hours' interrogation, Blunt never told Wright (or anyone else) about what he found in Germany. Possibly, like Coco Chanel, he knew that a promise to keep quiet about the papers would ensure his own immunity from prosecution.

Whether intended or not, the refusal to accept that the Windsors were Fascists has gone on and on. The 'Great Love Story' has appeared on television, and in numerous books. Experts argue about the psychology of the King, the ambition of Wallis Warfield, the hypocrisy of the British Establishment, the size of Edward's penis, and whether or not he was a foot-fetishist. All these matters are marvellous for serialisation in the *Daily Mail*, which itself enthusiastically supported the Fascists in the Thirties. Michael Bloch's *Secret File of the Duke of Windsor*, the latest in this genre (inevitably serialised in the *Daily Mail*), has but four references to Hitler and continues in the traditional view that the Duke was naive.[†] He thought, Bloch suggests, that the Nazis were 'rough but reasonable men', and underestimated their barbarism. Charles Higham has an answer to this: 'The repeated absurdity of journalists that the couple's commitment to Fascism and a negotiated peace in World War Two was based upon a transcendent foolishness stood exposed the moment one entered a conversation with the Windsors. Whatever one might think of their views, those views were not entered into lightly or from a position of blind ignorance.'

Wallis did not want to be the Duchess of Windsor. In personal terms, she preferred her tedious and undemanding husband Ernest Simpson to the ever-whining, introspective and hypochondriacal Duke. She wanted to be mistress to the King, not the wife of an exiled duke. She begged the King to stand by his throne, seeing herself as a modern Mrs Fitzherbert, in charge of the court but not of the court, enjoying all the pomp and influence of a queen without being the Queen. This desire was not inspired by straightforward social ambition: it came from her anxiety to influence the course of political events. The story, in short, is not just soppy sexist trash, as portrayed in the *Daily Mail*. It is a political melodrama of the highest consequence.

One of the weaknesses of modern republican theory is that it

[†] Bantam, 1988.

tends to concentrate on the personal weaknesses of the Royals. How could anyone, it is asked, support a system which raises on a pedestal people like Edward VIII or George IV or Andy and Fergie? Are they not absurd, ridiculous figures, unfit for anything but a jewellery auction or a hunt ball? This argument always falls flat. The influence of a monarchy which has long ago been stripped of real political power lies precisely in its absorption of people's aspirations, griefs, ambitions and endeavours. Weaknesses, therefore, are as adorable as strengths. Princess Diana has no O levels – so what? Nor have most other people. Fergie is a mindless Sloane with nothing but a cheerful grin – so what?

A cheerful grin is no bad thing when most people aren't feeling at all cheerful. Royal idiocies, divorces, selfishnesses, as detailed in the popular press, are not destructive of modern monarchy. On the contrary, they provide a vital link between the monarchs and their subjects.

So it was with the Windsors. The King of England fell for a divorced woman and beastly old Baldwin wouldn't let him have her. How rotten of him! How many others have fallen for unsuitable partners, but have not had their jobs taken away from them because of it? So it was that the people maintained their sympathy for the 'gallant young Prince'. The one quality of the Duke of Windsor which might have broken the spell of the British monarchy – his Fascist leanings – was discreetly buried.

Charles Higham's is an important book. But there is a great deal wrong with it. He has provided his critics with plenty of hostages. Again and again, he quotes the most scurrilous and unlikely gossip, without proving it. It is no good quoting one contemporary hazarding a guess that Wallis was the lover of Count Ciano, and that she even had an abortion as a result. There is not the slightest proof of this, and anyway it is beside the point. It is no good inventing (or guessing at) Wallis's sexual education in the brothels of Shanghai or for that matter entering the royal bedchamber to speculate about what exactly went on there. There are times – far too many of them – when bald assertions are not backed by the evidence they need; the notes and the index are a disgrace; and Higham's biographical method, piling incident on incident and referring only to the day and the month, continually loses the thread of the narrative.

But these are really niggles. Gossip is a dangerous commodity, but no biography worth its salt could survive without it. The plain fact is that for all its weaknesses the book is enthralling from first to last and for one central reason. It exposes both its main subject and her royal catch, not as the dim-witted, self-obsessed lovers who have been pickled for posterity, but as nasty, determined Fascists who wanted to preside over a 'new social order' which would do away for ever with all pretence at democracy and consign all opposition to the holocaust.

15 September 1988

Ghosts in the Palace

Tom Nairn

THE FIRST BRITISH ELECTION ever without the Monarchy: is this not how it's likely to be remembered? The Italian phrase for it is better than ours: *perdere la bussola*, the loss not merely of bearings but of the compass itself. Queen Elizabeth II will still be around for the vote, I know, but as little more than an accusing spectre. Within less than half of her own reign the glamour of Monarchy has vanished. All that the Crown now accomplishes is to counterpoint and somehow exaggerate an ambient unreality: the new, motherless country left behind by its moral decease. Through Queenly spectacles the past looks at the shattered glass of Britain present, with a gaze already cold.

A certain frigidity is in order, since it is actually a distinctively Royal sense of nationhood which has been thrown overboard. But too little attention has been paid to all the identity-accoutrements which have gone with it. Better British yesterdays, for example. This is the real trouble with Conservatism: its identity-bedrock has dissolved. Old-Brit nostalgia has found for itself a kind of foreign country, the one where things were done differently. Tories are as little at home there as anybody else. The past turns out to have been institutional in character, and not, as so often thought, an aspect of ethnic English character. When deep-set presuppositions are discarded in this way, those who have relied too heavily on them have to 'go mad'. Over-individualism, selfishness, loads-a-loot, heedlessness, wilfulness, everything now packaged as 'sleaze', move irresistibly into the vacuum. This happened first of all inside the Royal Family itself. It quickly extended from the head down to the gills, to the 'natural party of government'. People wanted to believe the trouble came from the personal quirks of younger Royals like Di and Fergie. In fact, personalities who would once have been safely suffocated or rendered decorous by Establishment guardians found easy voice among the loosening stays of the enterprise culture. The alteration had nothing to do with 'human nature' in general: all it vented was a British national character too long compressed and deformed by class responsibilities and alibis.

The monarchical nature invented in Victorian times was ballast as well as guidance-system: as conservatives (meaning pretty well everybody) used to say, it did make up for such a lot. It was a hallmark of fairness as well as grandeur, the national tea-ceremony, hierarchy's human face, balm for the marginalised. From that set of attitudes the over-celebrated sense of continuity and permanence was derived, the identity which was argued for by Edmund Burke but not really in existence until well after 1832. Once up and running it posed as immemorial, but actually it has lasted for about a century and a half. Thatcherism was its terminal disease. Enforced rejuvenation of the economic body destroyed a head far too dependent on forged antiquity and protocol. During its hegemony the second nature of regal possession was never just the mixture of theatre and contrivance depicted by philistines like Walter Bagehot. It was more like an identity-fabric which, in the odd conditions of Empire-Britain, stood in for other forms of nationalism.

With only a few years of hindsight it is obvious how such a moral structure can vanish far more utterly than places and buildings. Majorism was like an interminable funeral rite. Alan Bennett isn't alone in feeling that there's something deeply uncouth about this mutation: general melancholia and regret might indeed be more seemly for the old state-nation. Yet, as the famous Carlton TV programme on the Monarchy earlier this year showed, there is no chance of that: the wake naturally takes the form of a raucous, invigorating, escalating, would-be democratic row – itself entirely at odds with the spiritual ethos of yesteryear. The phone-in poll following the on-screen fisticuffs showed that overt republicanism had increased by only several hundred per cent, not yet enough for a majority in England. But in Scotland the dreadful had already happened. Not only was there a republican majority, but the once loyal *Scotsman* was falling into the grip of Andrew Neil, one of the brashest anti-Royal voices in the Carlton debate. Most commentary about the programme was fearfully disapproving: crass, vulgar, ill-judged, a 'tasteless screaming-match' and so on. The Independent Television Commission later supported such genteel verdicts, decreeing that it 'could not be regarded as a programme of high quality'. No, thank Christ, the audience did seem positively 'out of control', the pundits were not granted nearly enough time and even the telephone voting system contributed cheerfully to the chaos. But all that the row demonstrated was that broadsheet commentators and committee-folk have not yet shaken off old-order habits: they dwell still in a universe where the highest possible quality alone befits Royalty, and debates should be run by and for chaps. Oiks should express opinions only when requested under the appropriate fail-safe mechanisms: first-past-the-post voting is better than they deserve. I couldn't help feeling also that some of these notables must have forgotten what the old days were really like. This may be another feature of the bizarre transition now under way: once an over-starched taboo-culture has collapsed, within a short time surprisingly few can recall how it felt and functioned.

Back in the Sixties, for example, the *Scotsman* had a faithful operative entrusted with a quite peculiar task. When a Royal photo was to appear in the next day's paper he was handed the negatives well in advance and asked to eliminate too-prominent wrinkles or blemishes from the faces of Majesty. Off he would go to toil with sets of tiny brushes and jars of off-whitener, in a special darkroom somewhere in the basement of the newspaper's weird Neo-Gothic premises on Edinburgh's North Bridge, to forge a series of possible images for editorial approval. They had to be just right. This was glamour-enhancement where subtlety was all, the opposite of crass photo-vérité. Old Ukania thought it could still teach the Commies a thing or two. True iconisation was quite different from the over-obvious clean-up jobs being stamped out every day in Moscow and Tirana. The goal of Great Britain was maintenance of belief, not crass assertion of power. Taboos gratefully supported by the tabooed themselves: such was our way of doing things, clearly deserving help from responsible journalism. The overall result was that weird and now half-forgotten world of strangulated put-downs and place-knowing, the land of done things and seemly gestures in which nobody could say a serious word against Royalty and hence, by the oneiric subterranean logic of Britishness, not against continuity, permanence, wigs, Mr Speaker, fox-hunting, the Commonwealth or sovereignty either.

Yet it is in the nature of taboos to be broken: they are founded on custom and tradition, not democracy. In the UK they were a substitute for democracy as well as nationalism. Once smashed up by the Thatcherite wave-machine they fell immediately beyond redemption, and good riddance to them. The future we have to get on with is different. So let's start by treating the Royals as ghosts. Yes, we did once love them truly, madly, deeply; but Anthony Minghella's Zeitgeist movie didn't just argue that after-images may – perhaps even should – come back to haunt us. The point, surely, was that their sole utility should then be as midwives of a new start, a time that will allow them to cease hanging about, and depart with a sort of honour.

As things stand just now, would-be post-Brits have little chance of emulating that happy ending. Not, at least, for as long as there are so many utterly unghostlike Windsor presences still among us, sweating to keep the show on the road. All they are likely to achieve from now on is the annoyance of other road-users, but that doesn't seem to deter them. Once drained, a principally symbolic greatness can only turn into a burden, and before long into an irritant, and then into a source of division. For the Royals, to be costed was to be found wanting. It was often noticed at the time how Thatcher was always competing with Queen Elizabeth. An *Independent* story the other week related how, since being ennobled, she has even appropriated the Royal insignia for her notepaper. However, Thatcher was like King Midas in reverse. Everything she touched was magically transformed into lead: a metered liberty, the lowest common denominator of coinage. For the golden refulgence of Monarchy this was fatal. Something which ceases being priceless can only appear absurdly pricey. Is this what taxpayers were paying out for – not fairyland, only a cost-effective national showcase? Paying some income tax and charging for visits to Buckingham Palace simply compounded the offence. 'Good for tourism' is the most pitiable of defences. It turns Majesty into something good for a bob or two, alongside airport boutiques, Madame Tussauds, Travel Inns and the grazing herd of Royal biographers. Once upon a time the Royal Family was supposed to be good for us. Good, one now struggles to recall, in the sense of honourable, and ennobling to the collective consciousness.

I never felt sorry for them for the old reasons – no privacy, born to serve – but must admit to a few stirrings nowadays. For symbols to survive the evaporation of their meaning is shaming for us, but worse for them. In the dishonoured and nameless country where Britfolk will soon be voting, republicanism has become no more than anticipatory Grace: let a secular Mercy take care of these souls, and remove them from our daily sight. They used to emanate a stuffy, stilted and yet reassuring sense of familial continuance. Within the same spectrum of meaning lay their boringness, philistine cheeriness and all the rest of the taken-for-granted societal glue. But it all hung together: no one could now stand the stuffiness and class oppressiveness, and this means they can't have 'God bless'em!' and the sense of wonder either.

On the party-political side it may indeed be that whatever guarantees against lunacy a monarchy furnished have fallen off the cart as well. We can't be sure about this yet, in the darkling subsidence of Majorism. However, John Redwood, Sir George Gardiner and Michaels Howard and Portillo are scarcely arguments against the view. 'The source of the authority and legitimacy of government ... the personification of the nation ... an institution vital to our national well-being': once Portillo boomed his tawdry redemptionist eulogy of the Royals in 1994, they should have been on the first plane out. A political campaign to 'revive Monarchy' is the worst possible news for Prince Charles, Nicholas Soames and the other trusties. It means the game is really over. They will never be taken for granted again. More recently, Major cranked out his own version of the Royal thousand-year thing, and everyone remarked how unlike Laurence Olivier he sounded. This was actually rather unfair. It is the whole echo-chamber of Anglo-Brit imagined community which has fallen away; today, I doubt whether even the greatest of hams could successfully replace it.

Fintan O'Toole posed the right question about the episode in the *Irish Times*: 'why, if British identity is so secure, does its pedigree have to be so fantastically exaggerated?' To compensate for Monarchy-deflation, I'm afraid. O'Toole concluded: 'The invented British nation (1707-1997) is ... in urgent need of re-invention ... and this is why the forthcoming election will be a turning-point. This may be one of those very rare elections fought not on the firm ground of finance but on the slippery and uncertain territory of how a country might go about finding its lost destiny.' A sociological theorist might make the point this way: though not necessarily visible on a day-to-day or party-political plane, the loss of a key identifying system can cause a profound malaise, at once social and psychic, which finds expression through all sorts of circuitous or 'irrational' channels – O'Toole's 'uncertain territory' is one explored with much reluctance, amid wilful backsliding, bouts of scapegoating, escapist brainwaves and aggressive apathy, in a strange atmosphere specific to the recently bereaved. I noted the new salience of rogues and chancers earlier. Anxiety-ridden liberation may sound like a contradiction in terms, and yet individuals and societies do live out such contradictions, at least for a time.

Royal socialism used to be kept in reserve for such bad moments: the old cart-horse of the Movement, responsible trade unionism rising to the occasion, beer and sandwiches at No 10, the ennoblement of protesters. But here, too, the paternalistic parade is no more. It was condemned under Kinnock, and Tony Blair delivered the coup de grâce. Amitai Etzioni and Geoff Mulgan's Demos have been upgraded to fill the community-relations slot which was once the Monarchy's by right. Of course democracy ought to have moved in to supplant the deficiencies of a fallimentary patrician order, but that's the whole point: it couldn't. The United Kingdom's earlier victories over successive waves of revolution had so co-opted and stunted democracy that now, when a crasser impulse was at last required, the internal resources were lacking. What was needed was a heedless, levelling, shouting-and-dancing brawl, Carlton's Monarchy programme on the stage of the whole UK; what we got was Blairism, an improvement on the class-bound Left but still lacking in the state-reforming energy the moment requires. Like Thatcher before him, Blair has cloaked a sharply intensified centralism in the rhetoric of devolution. What she claimed to be handing down was economic opportunity, through the individualism of the enterprise culture; he claims to be allowing harmless new forms of local government in Scotland, Wales, Ulster, and even in the English regions if they make a sufficient nuisance of themselves. Yet such granted empowerment may also be power retained, or even reinforced: sovereignty can in this way survive the decay and disgrace of our figurative sovereigns, the miserable blood-royals themselves. It is being rehoused in sovereign-presidents, Gaullist concentrations of holy state-magic who see elections mainly as opportunities to make phoney contracts and pledges, or for the people to display 'trust' in referenda. The end of Monarchy might turn out to be its apotheosis.

There is a contrary, republican direction. But it would depend on reforming the centre itself: changing the Commons and the state's whole way of doing business, the electoral system, the Second Chamber and so the national identity and place in the world – above all its place in the European Union. It would involve making an end of Ukanian sovereignty, the Geist, not just its current bearer – a revolutionary task, but one which, as McKibbin suggested, may already have been hamstrung by so much safety-first, such a host of concessions to the Thatcherite economic spreadsheet.

24 April 1997

About as Useful as
a String Condom

Glen Newey

TIME'S WHIRLIGIG, as one surly underling told another, brings in its revenges. For the Royal Family, 2002 went bad faster than an over-hung widgeon. In September the Prince of Wales emerged as a nuisance letter-writer, badgering Government ministers with green-ink missives about the Human Rights Act and the hunting ban, and moans that Cumbrian farmers got a worse deal than blacks and homosexuals. In November the Princess Royal got a criminal record after her pet pit bull gored a child (the dog escaped the chop thanks to the Princess's top-dollar brief). Even Prince William, once the press's golden boy, was reported to have dispatched flunkeys to buy him porno mags from the local newsagent. Then came bruits of rape within the precincts of Buckingham Palace, and reports that the Royals' London flop-houses doubled as totters' yards for laundering swag ('Del Boy Royals' was the *Sun's* unimprovable headline). All this knocked the gilt off the 'Golden' Jubilee.

During the last big snafu concerning the Windsors, after the death of Diana, the main charge against the Royals was 'aloofness'. All this really amounted to was that they had shown themselves indifferent to the fate of a drama queen whose early death spared us all a lot of tedium. Now, however, the charges include subverting the administration of criminal justice, tax evasion,

squandering public money and undermining democracy. Once
the Burrell and Brown/Havlik trials collapsed, the finger pointed
directly at the Sovereign herself, who emerged (depending on
one's preferred theory) as Machiavellian, culpably misinformed,
vindictive or simply gaga. Whatever the explanation, the upshot
is a mighty waste of public cash. It could scarcely be worse if the
Queen had been caught running drugs on the (£35,000 per out-
ing) Royal train or if the Duke of Edinburgh had been pleasuring
corgis in Windsor Great Park.

Monarchophiles had talked up the Windsors' return to public
affection after the Jubilee, as if it were the happy end to a foolish
tale of republican flirtation. The last ten years have been a bum
decade for the Royals. Phone taps revealed that the heir-appar-
ent, previously thought to be interested in nothing more risqué
than the *Goon Show* and chats with root vegetables, aspired to be
his mistress's jam-rag. His younger son, third-in-line Prince Harry, was busted after splitting a splifferooney or three with low-
life cronies, and packed off to a suitably downmarket rehab bin.
Although public indignation at the burgeoning Civil List led to
some drastic pruning, the Royal supernumeraries continued to
live high on the hog. When the public purse snapped shut, they
resorted to ever more mercenary ways of earning a crust. Where-
as the Royals' rent-a-nob biz had previously been confined to
minor scions of the dynasty, the clampdown on the Saxe-Coburg
benefit scam brought it much closer to home. In an effort to
drum up business for her PR firm, Sophie, 'Countess of Wessex'
sounded off about the Prime Minister's wife to a couple of *News of
the Booze* hacks posing as Middle Eastern sheikhs. Then, following the brouhaha about 'media intrusion' on Prince William's arrival as a student at St Andrews University, it turned out that the
Prince had indeed been stalked – by his uncle's TV crew.

Until the June roisterings, 2002 had, by general consent, been
another annus horribilis. Nothing as bad as the Windsor Castle

fire, let alone the nasty arrival of a tax demand from the Inland Revenue on the Queen's doorstep a few years back; but it had nonetheless seen the deaths, within a few weeks of each other, of the Queen's 'much loved' sister and of her mother. Of course everybody had been expecting Mustique Meg and 'the Problem' (the Queen's affectionate soubriquet for her mother) to peg it for any number of years, and the QM's one benefaction to the nation – which got nothing in inheritance tax – was to croak over Easter, elbowing Jesus out of the TV schedules. Meanwhile the Prince Consort's capacity to goof remains undimmed by age. On the Jubilee tour of the UK the Duke picked out a blind woman from a crowd of 'well-wishers' and asked her if she knew that there are now 'eating dogs for the anorexic'.

In the background, of course, lay the fluff-ball Jacobinism of September 1997 which surfaced in the media after Diana's tryst with the underpass. It was rightly observed that the blood Royals inhabited an emotional tundra, where feeling was subjugated to 'duty' and 'the Firm'. By contrast, Diana had 'soul'. She bared all about self-harm and her frequent calls, during her bulimic phase, on the great white telephone. She fondled children and animals, dabbled in New Age pursuits, kibitzed in operating theatres and had been stiffed on a pedalo by the thick-set offspring of a Levantine grocer. In op-ed fable she presented the Windsor family's lone human face, Avon Lady to the House of Atreus.

This wasn't so long ago, and the Royals' supposed bounce back to public favour came as a shock to many in the commentariat. They need not have been surprised. Even in December 1997, at the supposed nadir of the Windsor clan's popularity, and the zenith of Tony Blair's, the Prime Minister's approval rating in a MORI poll was, at 61 per cent, the same as that for Prince Charles, detested ex-spouse of the Althorp Madonna and prime scapegoat for her death. Even immediately after the Paris shunt, a mere 18 per cent thought that Britain should dump the Royals in favour of a republic. This was hardly surprising: as mother to the heir-but-one to the throne Diana could reasonably be thought to have had a strong interest in the monarchy's survival. The republican upsurge was never a big deal.

Nonetheless, the 'perception' remains that for Royalists the Jubilee marked a reversal of fortune after the travails of the 1990s. In 2001 the dependably vacuous Jonathan Freedland gazed into his crystals and prognosticated that it was

> going to be so different this time – even the folks in Buckingham Palace are saying it. Next summer's Golden Jubilee, marking fifty years since Elizabeth II's Coronation, will not be the national jamboree and mass outpouring of affection that courtiers remember from 1977. It will be a modest, understated affair: a tasteful celebration for those who want it.

In the event, of course, the jamboree was about as modest, understated and tasteful as Liberace in a snakeskin posing pouch. How did 'the folks in Buckingham Palace' so easily squash Freedland's expectations? A clue comes from the neo-Bourbonesque rhetoric about the 'People's Monarchy' – the phrase harks back to one used by the Prime Minister on the morning Di went off to the great couturier in the sky. Blair's articulation of the 'national mood' easily outmanoeuvred the Opposition, whose hapless leader could only suggest that Diana give her name to Heathrow Airport: a better candidate would have been the Channel tunnel. Even then the 'People's Princess' was not merely an oxymoron, but a second-hand one at that. The phrase was coined by the dreck columnist and penny dreadful author Julie Burchill, who in Diana's later years cast herself in the role of damp-knickered schoolgirl to Di's dashing gym mistress.

Even so, the People's Princess tag stuck. Not least among the reasons for the label's durability is the Government's deployment of 'the People' to rebrand anything for which it wishes to suborn approval – witness the 'People's Lottery', the 'People's Dome' (at least before it succumbed to the People's apathy), the creation of 'People's Peers' and the former Culture Secretary's Goebbelsesque pronouncement that the arts 'must be relevant to the People'. The People now find themselves recruited to rubber-stamp whatever outcomes the vagaries of the market throw up – and indeed the market itself, which is with us, after all, by popular demand.

And so we come to the Jubilee and its reaffirmation of the 'People's Monarchy'. Before the day few thought that on 3 June a million or two groupies would throng the Mall to watch a bunch of clapped-out old-stagers presuming on the public's indulgence for one last hurrah. But so it proved. When Diana bought the farm only a few months into his Premiership, Blair was still able to pose as the champion of the *petit peuple* against the forces of reaction: that is, old privilege, money and the establishment. The blame-fest which followed her death put the Royals in the dock for the beatified Princess's demise. The tabloids condemned them, not unfittingly, as the curdled dregs of an outmoded caste. By contrast, the Princess was celebrated as 'modern', a tag which the New Labour 'Project' had already collared. The monarcho-phile Blair had, to be sure, to tread carefully, since his strategy of siding with the wailing Dianistas risked toppling the Royals once and for all. His great coup during the week between Diana's death and funeral was to keep up this pose while rescuing the Palace from the spectre of black republicanism, in the face of both a snarling press and a po-faced sovereign who couldn't see what the fuss was about. By the end of the week, though, Number Ten had convinced even Her Majesty that without a sop to sentiment this could be the Big One, and had scripted her some old-balls lines for telecast ('as a grandmother' etc) which answered the call for gush.

Things are different now. Mishaps too numerous and familiar

to mention have blotted the Dear Leader's credentials as a tribune of the People. Over the last five years New Labour has grafted itself seamlessly to the rootstock of the reaction it once claimed to abhor. The People's Premier has shown himself to be Lakshmi Mittal's Premier, Bernie Ecclestone's Premier, George W. Bush's pet puff-adder – the hireling, in short, of anyone with power or ready cash. While this glad-handing was politically motivated, we now also know that the Blairs are not above schmoozing with conmen for real-estate discounts. The old adage has it that British prime ministers are either vicars or bookmakers. In Phoney Tony the country has a bookie masquerading as a vicar, a posture that does little for the standing of either profession. As a result Blair has lost his claques. He has toadied to those, including the Queen, whose affection for him cannot be relied on to last longer than next week's polls.

Seen in this light, the question why the Queen made a 'comeback' with the Jubilee junket answers itself. In cahoots with the media, the Palace turned the tables on Number Ten. Nowadays it's the Royals, not the New Labour nomenklatura, who are prolier than thou, and the true custodian of the public weal. The media's claim that the PM had 'muscled in' on Royal grief during the Queen Mother's funeral completed his fall from divine emissary to scourge of Black Rod, as Blair was charged with milking the photo-op to improve his own image. But to ask why the Royals suddenly found themselves on the up and up is to miss the point. The most interesting question concerning the monarchy is how, given its absurdity, the institution manages to stagger on, even posing on occasion as the voice of the dispossessed. Behind this is the unignorable dilemma besetting third-millennium monarchy. How can the existence of the hugely rich and not-so-powerless Windsors be squared with democratic ideals of political and civic equality?

Before the Jubilee the dilemma may have looked insoluble.

One proposal was that the Queen should slum it a bit more, perhaps through a spot of biking – the so-called Dutch model of monarchy. Further possibilities for down-marketing readily suggest themselves: the monarch could do something seriously common, like getting a nipple pierced or presiding over 'Royal Big Brother' at a palace in an undisclosed location. Flailing attempts have, of course, been made in this direction, such as the Queen's much trumpeted 'pub visit' in Devon five years ago, when she eyed a jar of the local brew as if it were a vial of rat's piss. No doubt her failure to sample it owed more to a heartfelt aversion to her subjects' tipple of choice than to political calculation. Even so, the underlying instinct is quite correct: that she becomes less majestic the more she sluts out, and monarchy without majesty is about as useful as a string condom.

Another way for the Royals to respond to the dilemma would be to insist on their difference from the Great Unwashed. This certainly chimes better with the Queen's own view of the world, in which even the corgis eat out of solid silver bowls. But it meets with no more success than going déclassé, the obvious problem being that old-style deference has – at least on the plane of rhetoric – gone for good. Admittedly, the monarchy has proven adept, down the centuries, at the old divide-and-rule ploy. Offering mediocrities the chance to scramble a few inches up the greasy pole while trampling on those beneath is a splendid way to shore up hierarchy. But the class society is no longer rhetorically respectable. After all, the Government came to power in 1997 pledged to end the 'absurdity' of conferring political power by heredity (a stance which it took to apply to the House of Lords but not the monarchy). The *Daily Mail*'s continuing outrage that the 'Michaels' can squat Kensington Palace for a rent that wouldn't cover a bus shelter anywhere else in the borough (defending his lifestyle, Prince Michael protested that 'it's paid for by us – except the house, clearly') shows that the wraith of monarchomachy can pop up anywhere. Attempts to reaffirm an old hierarchy in rhetoric as well as reality risk the dread charge of 'elitism'.

As with so many dilemmas, one way to deal with this one is by not thinking about it much. This displays, in John Dunn's apt phrase, the cunning of unreason. The alternative is to embrace doublethink. We, the People, are the democratic sovereign: it is by popular demand that the monarch rules over us, her subjects. Or, the Queen is naturally our better, but like the jellied-eel-and-brown-ale-guzzling Queen Mother, she is also one of us. The Queen costs a bargain 58p per subject per annum to maintain (this was the positive spin put on the revelation last year that the true cost of the monarchy – £35million – was considerably higher than previously acknowledged), but is, of course, worth anything between £50m and £350m, and benefits from sundry perks and tax breaks. She is a mere 'figurehead', but wields at least some form of power as head of the Commonwealth, head of the Armed Forces, head of the established Church and head of the Privy Council. She is entitled to give or withhold assent from democratically enacted legislation and to dissolve Parliament, and is entitled to an hour's free ear-time each week with the Prime Minister, over whom she uniquely has the prerogative of hire and fire. She is the German-descended, and her progeny the Graeco-German-descended, epitome of Englishness. Accordingly, though she reigns as Queen of all her subjects, she can't legally marry a Catholic, and wouldn't have married anyone black or Asian, or anyone else much below the rank of Viscount, the thought of Papist or mongrelised or demi-prole heirs to the Throne being beyond imagination. The only reason she and her kin play the role of figureheads to the nation more plausibly than a president created by election or lot is that, as a clan riven by estrangement, multiple divorce, adultery, alcoholism and sporadic psychosis, they exemplify actual family values.

Not thinking about the dilemma does not, of course, get rid

of it. The Royals remain strung between coming out as poshness incarnate and getting back in the closet by masquerading as proles. Hence the epiphany of a bemused monarch and her consort watching the antics of Brian May on top of her own strobe-lit Palace on 3 June. Hence, also, the most arresting spectacle of royal conflagration since the storming of the Winter Palace, the pyrotechnic finale of the schlock extravaganza cannibalising the very imagery of revolt. The Royals' accommodation with popular culture had, however, already gone further than this. Soon after the Queen Mother's death the nation learned that she had been a devotee of Ali G. Apparently, after a bottle or two of Beefeater the old girl would snap her fingers and mimic his catch-word ('respec") to the amusement of her great-grandsons. Those in the Palace press office who placed this story in the papers presumably recalled the scene in *Ali G: Indahouse* where Ali learns that the Queen shaves her pubes, and can manage only to repeat his catch-word in awe. There isn't much ground left for dissent to occupy when royaldom eagerly appropriates even lèse-majesty about the reginal jock-region.

As the Jubilee showed, there's been no reduction in the rhetorical value of the People in gilding the masque of power. The telly plugs for the Jubilee bash made this plain. In the commercials, a caricature toff supposedly in the royal employ (Rowan Atkinson, in his *Blackadder* persona) schemes to stifle the Palace schlock-rock gig at its birth. But we – that is, we the People – know that his knavish tricks will be frustrated and that the mystic bond between Sovereign and People will be sealed through our shared devotion to the music of Ozzy Osbourne. To describe this as playing both ends against the middle would be to miss the fictive quality of the middle, and the dominance of one end over the other. It makes of the People a ventriloquist's dummy and passes off as their collective will a script drafted and spoken for them by those who aim to remain their betters.

Commentators sometimes portray this monarcho-syndical-ism as a coalition against capitalism, a pseudo-Tawneyite rerun of the Middle Ages. But the lines of allegiance can run either way, since capital's apologists like to pretend that companies such as Enron and WorldCom – sleights of the invisible hand – come to us by popular demand. In any case, it is a myth that royalty and capitalism don't mix. The first anniversary of Diana's death saw an effluent-stream of memorabilia, coffee-table books and the like, including commemoration plates which tootled out a ren-dition of 'Candle in the Wind' at the press of a button, assorted effigies and, reportedly, a commemorative seat-belt issued by an enterprising German auto-parts firm. The Golden Jubilee was marked by the issue of a limited-edition dildo embossed with the royal crest, presumably designed to concentrate the minds of Albion's daughters (and sons) as they gaze at the ceiling and wax nostalgic over Empire.

What's more, there is a symbiotic relation between monarchy and the form of democracy that exists in Britain. Governments use the Royals as handy whipping-boys when the peasants grow disgruntled, or as a decoy to draw popular fire when Westmin-ster power and privilege seem overweening. The honours system doles out cheap gongs to underpaid public servants and buys off dissidents – consider Harold Pinter's recent CH, or David Hare's K. Conversely, the Royals are happy to benefit from the disre-pute into which democratic politics habitually brings itself. This is particularly useful when, as now, politicians' mendacity and self-interest meets with public 'cynicism' and the discrediting of democracy: by 'transcending politics', the monarchy serves to defang revolt and contain it within the system. As a pre-demo-cratic throwback, the tribal elders are well placed to fill the fidu-ciary void.

Admittedly, their power to plug the credibility gap may be temporarily sapped by the monarch's sabotage of the criminal justice system over which she presides, her paying as little tax as she can to the state she heads, the van-loads of gifts her brood apparently hawks for ready cash, and whatever fresh scandals this year may bring. An episode in which the Queen was happy to see a faithful servant go to the wall until a word from the Dauphin made her aware of the beans about to be spilled, and was no less insouciant at the waste of public money when memory resumed its sway, in the end produced not much more than a clacking of the chatterati's worry-beads. The Royals may, in the way of families, be primitive, grasping and sadistic. But they're our own, and we cannot but love them.

To all appearances, the political views of the People's Monarch and her family suit their role admirably, and guarantee their survival for decades, maybe centuries, to come. The Queen's own political philosophy can only be guessed at, but given her standing as the UK's – perhaps the world's – richest woman, it is unlikely to include a vision of society in which power and wealth are distributed more equitably. All surviving evidence about the political views of the Queen Mother indicates that she couldn't have got much further rightwards without buying a uniform. The most that can be extracted in the way of political content from the Prince of Wales's rambling public pronouncements is a blathering eco-feudalism in which society is an idealised Highgrove. For the political philosophy of the Prince Consort, and in particular his views on popular sovereignty, we need look no further than his encounter with General Alfredo Stroessner, who between 1954 and his overthrow in 1989 ran what amounted to a sunset home for ageing Nazis in Paraguay. On a trip to Asunción before the General got the heave-ho, the Duke told him: 'It's a pleasant change to be in a country that isn't ruled by its people.' The Duke needn't have left home.

23 January 2003

Short Cuts

Thomas Jones

IT MAY BE that by the time this issue of the LRB is published, the monarchy-obliterating secret that lurks on Fleet St will have been revealed and the last of the Windsors will be preparing for exile in Bermuda, or some other far-flung corner of their former realm: Port Stanley, say, or Balmoral. Paul Burrell will have packed their bags for them one last time. The 'irony' of which, as Burrell would say (the only words that he misuses more often are 'surreal' and 'enormity'), is that he's a die-hard monarchist, as he reveals in his memoir, A Royal Duty, a book at once agonisingly boring and shamefully fascinating.* Much the most interesting bits are the insights into such things as what the Queen has (or used to have) for breakfast: 'one slice of granary toast, a smear of butter and a thin layer of dark, chunky marmalade', since you ask. She enters her dining-room every morning prompt at nine o'clock, 'carrying her old-fashioned Roberts radio tuned permanently to BBC Radio 2'. One of her two personal footmen (Burrell, from April 1978 to August 1987) butters the toast, but she makes her own Earl Grey tea, in a silver teapot, with water boiled in an electric kettle. I was rather impressed by her mucking in like this, until I learned (not from Burrell) that it's one of the many royal traditions started by George III. Shortly before one o'clock, she 'often made herself a large glass of her favourite pre-luncheon tipple, gin and Dubonnet, in equal half measures,

---

* Michael Joseph, £17.99.

with two lumps of ice and a slice of lemon'. I don't suppose this practice originated with George III, but you never know. Burrell once entered the royal sitting-room, 'late at night, not long before bedtime, and there she sat, in a smart silk dress in her chair at the desk near the window. She was wearing the Imperial State Crown. And her pink mule slippers.' She wasn't revelling in being Queen just for the hell of it, but getting accustomed to the weight of the crown for the State Opening of Parliament the next day: at least, that's what she told Burrell.

After he'd left Buckingham Palace to work for the Prince and Princess of Wales, the Queen rang Highgrove one day to speak to her son, as mothers do. The butler, as butlers do, answered the phone. 'Hello Paul,' she said. 'Good morning, Your Majesty,' he replied, before launching into a series of questions about the state of the Queen's health and how the corgis were, remembering no doubt the many happy hours that he and the Queen had spent together on their hands and knees, feeding the dogs their cough medicine. 'Is His Royal Highness there?' she interrupted. Burrell realised he 'had obviously talked too long'. He persists, however, in the belief that he and the Queen had a special, personal relationship, when it's pretty evident, from his own account, that his ardent feelings for her weren't entirely reciprocated. Burrell has a thing for women in positions of authority, and not just the Queen and Diana. Mrs Justice Rafferty, who presided over his trial, fascinated him, too: she was 'the image of elegance', 'far too glamorous to be a judge'.

The heir to the throne leaves memos rather than talking to his staff in person, asking them to do things such as rummage through his wastepaper basket for a mislaid letter from the Queen. He has a special silver device, like a small sardine-key, for squeezing out his toothpaste. Whether Charles squeezes it out himself, or gets his valet to do it for him, Burrell doesn't say. Once, at Balmoral, when Burrell was still a footman, Charles 'stood in the hall and shouted for assistance'. Burrell came running, to see 'two giant salmon' at the Prince's feet, which he was instructed to take to the kitchen. He didn't know how to pick them up. 'Prince Charles watched me juggling pathetically with them. "Oh, come here!" he said impatiently. "Don't mess around. Look." He took one of my hands, and pushed two of my fingers deep into its gills. I thought I was going to pass out.'

If Charles is more comfortable handling cold fish, Diana couldn't have been snugglier with her devoted butler. Maybe they were close friends; maybe she was needy and manipulative; maybe it was a bit of both. She wasn't shy of reminding him who was boss (he calls her 'the Boss'). There's a revealing story about going to see *Don Quixote* at the Royal Opera House. Burrell hadn't been to the ballet before. When, back at the palace, Diana asked his opinion, he told her he thought it was amazing, then asked her what she thought. '"Rubbish," she said, and burst out laughing when she saw the surprise on my face.' Not that he seems to mind.

Waiting for the lift at Russell Square tube station, as I read Burrell's not quite breathtaking account of how he contemplated suicide in a lay-by off the A41, the woman standing next to me asked, in an accusing tone: 'Is that really worth the read?' I said that, surprisingly, it was, but added, like a coward, that I hadn't paid for the book. 'Nothing wrong with a bit of gossip,' she said. 'As long as it's harmless.' Over the last decade or so, the monarchy has been thought to be in danger on a number of occasions: the events that constituted the Queen's annus horribilis, the death of Diana, Burrell's trial, Burrell's book, and now the allegations that the *Mail on Sunday* wasn't allowed to print, which are this evening (6 November) being denied by the Prince of Wales. But it's not at all clear that the institution stands or falls according to the activities of its incumbents. Just because Paul Burrell can't distinguish the monarchy from the Windsors doesn't mean everyone else has to make the same mistake: the case for republicanism doesn't depend on the bad behaviour of members of the royal family. Their antics are a distraction from the larger questions – but no less enthralling for that.

20 November 2003

Squidging About

Caroline Murphy

AARON BARSCHAK, who gatecrashed Prince William's 21st birthday party last year, says the question he is most often asked is: 'What was Camilla Parker Bowles like?' He could do worse than refer the curious to Rebecca Tyrrel's book.★ Born on 17 July 1947 (she is 16 months older than Prince Charles), Camilla is the daughter of an army major, Bruce Shand, and a society hostess, the Honourable Rosalind Shand (née Cubitt). Her paternal grandfather, P. Morton Shand, was an 'insatiable Lothario', who married four times. At the time of his third divorce, in 1931, the High Court described him as 'a peculiarly shameless litigant'. On her mother's side, Camilla's relatives are racier still. Her great-aunt was Violet Trefusis, the lover of Vita Sackville-West. Even better, her great-grandmother, Alice Keppel, was Edward VII's official mistress. It may be more than mere chance that the role of maîtresse-en-titre to the Prince of Wales runs in the family. Tyrrel says that, as a child, Camilla not only knew about her ancestor's liaison but regarded the story as 'talismanic', and loved to brag about it to her schoolfriends.

Camilla's education was expensive, ineffective and bizarre. She attended a prep school called Dumbrells, where a 'large, crucified bat' hung in the entrance hall. This appears to have set the tone of the establishment, which was by all accounts spartan in its accommodation and draconian in its discipline. 'It was

---

★ *Camilla: An Intimate Portrait* (Short Books, 2003).

decreed,' one contemporary of Camilla's recalls, 'that any possession found lying about must then be worn by the culprit for a whole day, including mealtimes. One older girl came to lunch wearing three hats; a younger one was sadly hampered by a large sewing basket tied to her waist.'

After Dumbrells came Queen's Gate, an establishment that Camilla – armed with only one O level – left for finishing school in Switzerland. She is remembered by at least one Queen's Gate contemporary (Lynn Ripley, who went on to become a pop singer called Twinkle and to marry the man from the Milk Tray adverts) as 'the coolest girl in school', despite never ditching her 'twinsets and tweeds'.

An aspect of the 1960s that didn't pass Camilla by was sex. She was known, according to Tyrrel, for being 'raunchy and randy'. A nameless contemporary notes that Camilla – unlike her sister, Annabel – was very much the sort 'to throw her knickers on the table'. In 1966, when she was 19, the knicker-throwing debutante met a 27-year-old lieutenant in the Guards, Andrew Parker Bowles. He was handsome, and his parents were 'excellent in-law material'. His father, Derek, a steward at Newbury racecourse, was a great friend of the Queen Mother's, while his mother, Ann (nicknamed 'Rhino'), was the Chief Commissioner of the Girl Guides. The only drawback was that Andrew was a womaniser. Lady Caroline Percy, one of his other girlfriends at this time, says that 'Andrew behaved abominably', but Camilla was 'desperate to marry him'. In 1970 Andrew took up with the 19-year-old Princess Anne: Tyrrel borrows from another royal biographer, Christopher Wilson, the speculation that 'it was to Andrew' that Anne 'surrendered her virginity'. It wasn't that Camilla was worried he might marry Anne (Andrew was Catholic and therefore out of the question) but that he had bagged the most high-profile catch available. Camilla had to do something spectacular to keep up. That summer, she chatted up Prince Charles at a polo match. 'He was a bigger royal with bigger prospects than Andrew's fling,' Tyrrel says, and 'he would have been looking pretty sweaty and macho post-chukka.' Camilla soon started seeing Charles whenever he wasn't off with the Navy, and Andrew whenever he wasn't off with the Army.

Charles had been encouraged, by Mountbatten and others, to have relationships with what Tyrrel calls 'sex-motherers' – nice, experienced girls with whom he could have sex without having to worry about the consequences. Camilla was meant to be one of these. Meanwhile, Andrew continued to see Princess Anne until she took up with Mark Phillips, which finally prompted Andrew to propose to Camilla. They married in June 1973. The news distressed Charles, who was at sea. 'I suppose the feeling of emptiness will pass eventually,' he wrote to Mountbatten, ruminating on what had happened to his 'blissful, peaceful and mutually happy relationship' with Camilla. What made her so special? She was, he later told his official biographer, Jonathan Dimbleby, a 'pretty' and 'bubbly' girl, who 'laughed easily and at the same sillinesses' as Charles himself. Tyrrel is more blunt. Camilla was, she says, a 'big-bosomed Goons fan'. But she clearly offered something more than this. Patty Palmer-Tomkinson is not the only friend of Charles and Camilla's to have observed that Camilla loves the Prince 'the way one loves a child'.

Whenever he was in England, Charles was a frequent visitor at Camilla's house, even when Andrew was at home. It was not unusual for guests at Parker Bowles dinner parties to spot the Prince waiting patiently for Camilla in the kitchen 'like a child'. He was, Tyrrel writes, 'like the Winslow Boy, arriving home unexpectedly out of the rain, wanting nanny to give him a hot bath, a milky drink and, in the Prince's case, a quick dip into her cleavage'.

Press speculation at the time about the women in Charles's life focused on 'leggy Sloanes' such as Sabrina Guinness and Lady Sarah Spencer. Had the papers only thought to look in Camilla's direction, they might have witnessed what one anonymous butler described seeing in her grandmother's garden – Charles and Camilla doing 'what Lady Chatterley enjoyed best'. Andrew did not object to the royal liaison: it kept the heat off his own affairs. Diana, however, was different: a virgin bride with no experience of the casually adulterous world in which her husband had lived as a bachelor, she naively expected monogamy.

Tyrrel questions whether Charles ever meant to give up Camilla when he married. For one thing, Camilla vetted Diana as she had done all Charles's would-be-wives. (Her vetting criteria are unclear. 'Was it their potential as a royal bride she was assessing,' Tyrrel asks, 'or was she gauging how much of a threat they might be to her own arrangement with Charles?') Then there was Highgrove. The house in Gloucestershire which Charles bought the year before his marriage was only 11 miles from the Parker Bowles's. In Diana's eyes it was 'bricks-and-mortar evidence of the colluding, of the fact that she had been duped'. But for all that Diana raged at Charles for his barely concealed relationship with Camilla, nothing changed. The collusion extended to the Prince's close circle of friends, who could be relied on for their discretion and their willingness to put their homes at Charles and Camilla's disposal. As Tyrrel has it, these large country houses were 'Charles and Camilla's very own Travelodges'. They were not as secure as they seemed, however: servants occasionally broke ranks. One miffed housekeeper told the *Daily Mirror*: 'After she's been staying, I find knickers all over the place.' That Camilla's knicker-throwing days were far from over was confirmed by a phone call Charles made to Camilla from one of these houses in 1989. Recorded by an anonymous snoop, the Camillagate tape came to light in 1993 (the year after the Queen's annus horribilis, which had seen, among other things, Charles and Diana's separation). The transcript was published all over the world. Fiji immediately announced that it would never again celebrate the Prince's birthday; the Italians called him 'Prince Tampaccino'.

The fall-out for Camilla was closer to home. Her husband wasn't happy about being the nation's best-known cuckold; her children were teased. Her son, Tom, the Prince's godson, 'was forced to listen to other boys at school reading the creepiest sections of the transcript out loud'. Camilla herself received hate-mail and crank calls. According to a friend, 'for a time she thought she was the most hated woman in the country.' She won sympathy in unexpected quarters, however. At the end of 1993, Spode produced a porcelain figurine called Camilla. It cost £165 and came with a 'heart-rending little story': 'She had a secret admirer, but strict social etiquette forbids her talking to him, or even acknowledging him.' Tyrrel doesn't tell us how well the figurines sold.

The Parker Bowles marriage survived the humiliation of Camillagate. But in June 1994 – against Camilla's wishes – Charles gave an interview to Jonathan Dimbleby. In response to the suggestion that his relationship with Camilla had caused the breakdown of his marriage, Charles said: 'all I can say is there's been so much speculation and feeding on every other kind of speculation so it all becomes bigger and bigger; but all I can say is, um . . . that, I mean, there is no truth in so much of this speculation, and Mrs Parker Bowles is a great friend of mine and I have a large number of friends.'

Although it upset the Scout Association, which has the Prince of Wales's feathers on its crest, and will have to pledge allegiance to him when he's king (it said that Charles did not represent the virtues the Association extolled of 'honesty, integrity and the sanctity of marriage'), the interview – against all press predictions other than Dimbleby's own – boosted Charles's popularity with the public. It signalled the end of the Parker Bowles marriage, however. Camilla was forced reluctantly back into the spotlight, and Andrew was 'galled and upset'. In January 1995, he and Camilla announced their divorce. Camilla moved to a new house in Wiltshire, only twenty minutes from Highgrove. One visitor described Ray Mill as 'just what Charles wants a home to be – comfortable, chintzy and a place to squidge about in'. It's a description that, in the light of the Camillagate tape, might apply to his mistress too.

22 January 2004

Tunnel Vision

Jenny Diski

I HAD SUPPER with a friend on 31 August 1997. He arrived looking wonderstruck. 'Are we just going to have dinner?' he said.

'Why, you think we should sit shiva?'

'But if she can die then anyone can.'

I don't think anyone else ever got around to articulating that quite so precisely.

One friend spent the day of the funeral in his study, locked away from the world, reading *Civilisation and Its Discontents*. Others I knew wandered around the flower carpet outside Kensington Palace, spying and sniffing the air to gauge whether sentimentality and hysteria actually might achieve what neo-Marxian analysis had failed to do in the 1960s and 1970s. Not being a great one for crowds, I stayed at home with the TV on, just watching and wondering at the events of that week, which really were strange on a scale beyond anything I'd encountered. Some months later, I saw a documentary made on the day of the funeral, in which a bag lady was asked for her opinion on the death of the Princess of Wales: 'Oh, she's died has she? I wondered why there were so many people about.'

Ten years on, with so many more screens and pages clogged with celebrity, and the broadsheets gone overtly tabloid, it isn't entirely obvious what fascinated people so about Diana Windsor, née Spencer, the uneducated, O-level-free daughter of an ancient house, former nanny, Sloane, clothes-horse, playgirl, campaigner, therapist addict. Take the bright lights away and you have a regular messy divorce, friends taking sides, money, adultery, using the kids. The only remarkable thing was that he left her for an older woman. The rest is pedestrian, and the fact that it was a royal divorce doesn't quite make up for the dullness of most of the characters involved. It was, perhaps, Princess Diana's contradictions that kept the interest alive. She spent £3000 a week on grooming and hugged lepers. She secretly visited centres for the homeless, taking her sons with her to ensure they learned about privilege, and issued an angry public statement when a tabloid picture showed a suggestion of cellulite on her thighs. But scrutinise the first 36 years of anyone's life and you will find no end of contradictions (with the possible exception of Paris Hilton's). It was just that for a brief period Diana had more and grander opportunities for contradictory behaviour than most of us. This might be what celebrity obsession is: watching and waiting for them to get all the usual things wrong, but on a monstrous scale. If we had access to the private life of God (and there's one who had opportunities and blew it) he'd be the celebridaddy of them all.

Only two factors count: the public has an appetite for the details of public lives that are supposed to be secret, and there are vast amounts of money to be made in giving it this information. What else is there to be interested in? What else can the media do but go on giving us what we're interested in? You can choose between helplessly watching rich, stupid folk walk into brick walls, and helplessly taking in the global suffering caused by politicians and corporations, and, of course, by our own greed. Better to be unable to do anything about something you don't really care about. So the books keep coming. They're still writing about Marilyn and Princess Grace: why, after only ten years, wouldn't we be deluged with books about Diana? It's just, you know, the way the world is.

Diana, as the first narrator of her own yarn, seemed to understand that stories have their own needs and immutable trajectories. Diana told Andrew Morton in *Diana: Her True Story* that she would never be queen. In 1992 I reviewed the Morton book for this paper and mocked her prediction: 'The premonition is never quite explained. Does she think that death is beckoning, or divorce, or is she planning to become a nun?' Well, aside from marrying Christ, that was exactly what she did think, and what, indeed, happened. In the *Panorama* interview of 1995, she told Martin Bashir that she believed she would die young. She wrote to her butler, in a letter to be published after her death, that there would be a nasty car crash, a head injury or something; that she would be got rid of. Diana had a respect for narrative rules that I quite lack, and narrative repaid her by enclosing her possessively in the story.

Diana Spencer, who wasn't keen on literature, being, as she said, thick as two planks, nonetheless spent her girlhood obsessively reading the books of her step-grandmother, Barbara Cartland. But she was better than Cartland, whose books invariably ended happily for their good girl heroines after a vicissitude or two. Diana understood the more compellingly modern psychological drama of the ineluctably unhappy ending for those who acted out, and did not or could not abide by the rules. She became an avatar of modernity, stepping boldly into her role as victim ('There were three of us in this marriage' and overdoing the kohl under her eyes), while fully complying with the requirements of the great amorphous conspiracy that keeps society on a roughly even keel (being easily dismissible as a hysteric and failing to wear a seat belt). With a better education, she might have liked Hardy and read Foucault with interest. 'She won't go quietly, that's the problem,' Diana said to 15 million people in the *Panorama* interview, slipping naturally into the third person. It was more like a trailer than a warning.

Still, you wonder, is there really anything more to say? The answer is no, but Tina Brown and Sarah Bradford soldier on nevertheless.* Each of them has produced hundreds of pages based on books already written (by journalists, her friends, his friends, butlers, nannies, ex-employers, protection officers, a speech trainer, lovers, paparazzi) and the odd interview with people who have already been interviewed for the books already written. They even quote one another. Certainly the material is almost identical in the two books. They consider the evidence that everyone else has considered and conclude as everyone else has concluded that there were faults on both sides and that the crash at the Pont d'Alma was a tragic accident.

Tina Brown has the social edge, however, on Sarah Bradford, the professional biographer who came to Princess Diana with her ladylike prose after books on such considerable women as the Queen, Jackie Kennedy and Lucrezia Borgia. As sometime editor of *Vanity Fair* and the *New Yorker*, Brown had a couple of lunches with Diana (Four Seasons, Anna Wintour, a charity do). Moreover, as she lists in her seven pages of acknowledgments, she knows all (two full pages) the right people (Lord Rothschild, Henry Kissinger, Bruce Oldfield, Emma Soames), quantities (three paragraphs) of the right researchers, and even the right London hotel owner, who made 'a room available every time I hit town' for 'a demanding writer with a moody computer' in his 'comfortable, centrally located and fashionably cool' hotel. The full list of books 'that have enriched this one' takes up four pages. And, doubtless with great relief because photo booths are so often out of order, she thanks, too, 'the gifted photographer Annie Leibovitz', who 'with her usual generosity insisted on taking the portrait the publisher required for my book jacket'.

In addition to all this, Brown has years of journalistic experience to draw on for her prose. It shows when she muses about Diana's final moments after Henri Paul arrived 'to drive her away

---

* *The Diana Chronicles* (Century, 2007); *Diana* (Penguin, 2007).

through celebrity's electric storm. Does she think then of her sons, asleep in a Scottish castle? As she slides quickly into the back seat of the Mercedes on that close Parisian night, does she suddenly miss the cool English rain?' Not that Brown is exclusively high-minded and lyrical, but for salacious gossip she has to rely on the likes of Gyles Brandreth, whom she quotes quoting Barbara Cartland on the failure of the royal marriage: 'Of course, you know where it all went wrong. She wouldn't do oral sex.'

Brown has her own views. Diana's timing was bad. 'Lady Diana Spencer took her bow at the nexus of a national malaise brought about by a sclerotic social-welfarism that had lost its way and an ever hotter press competition for royal stories.' I'm not sure whether this passing political analysis means that if Britain had had a privatised healthcare system such as the Americans rejoice in and had refused to assist the underprivileged then the tabloids would not have cared so much about the wayward princess. But Brown is clear that Diana fitted herself for a fairytale and then had nothing to wear when the emperor's clothes vanished. All the emotional intelligence in the world won't do if you think it's OK to hang out with the Fayeds. If only she *had* gone quietly, become the landmine queen of people's hearts, the dress-auctioning charitable divorcée, Blair's roving ambassador of love in a really hugging, mute, big-eyed, wildly successful, mint-green, tanned sort of way. 'I wish we could leave Diana's story there. I wish we could leave her as I saw her that summer's day in New York in her mint-green suit and early tan when she came for the wildly successful auction of her dresses.' Instead, she let herself down. It wasn't entirely her fault, Brown allows. It was a lack of love. That 'always dragged her down'. Her mother left her, her husband left her. She argued with and stopped speaking to her mother, her sisters, her brother, her friends. She nuisance-called boyfriends who were happy to be smuggled into Kensington Palace in the boot of her car but not to leave their wealthy wives, and then she had to go and fall in love with Hasnat Khan, who just wanted to be a good cardiac surgeon and marry the girl of his mother's dreams. She couldn't cope with the collapse of the Cartland fantasy almost-come-true; she had the breeding but not the reading.

Finally, though, the weight of Brown's argument seems to conclude that the descent into the tunnel was set in motion by her descent into bad taste, by being in the wrong place in the wrong season with the wrong people. Brown's great contribution to our understanding of the tragic end of the Princess of Wales depends on her knowledge of what's what in a world that the rest of us can only gawp at. Between her book's gynaecologically pink covers she straightens out her downscale readers on how low Diana had sunk that night in Paris as she left the Ritz:

> In August most upscale Parisians head north to Deauville for the polo and the racing or to the cool woods of their country estates in the Loire or Bordeaux ... Paris's most prestigious hotel at that time of the year is crawling with camera-toting tourists and rubber-neckers. At the end of the seasonal exit from town even the more exclusive areas of the hotel – such as its restaurant, L'Espadon – have a louche air of rootless extravagance. South American call girls with hirsute operators from emerging markets and rich old ladies with predatory nephews can be seen poring over the wine list.

Crawling, my dears. Pay attention, Tina's talking class here, and the price a girl pays when she lets herself down.

> For women over 35, glamour has three Stations of the Cross: denial, disguise and compromise. As she entered her 37th year Diana told herself she was looking for love. But what she was really seeking was a guy with a Gulfstream. Her needs at this juncture had more in common with those of second-act sirens like Elizabeth Hurley than with those of anyone currently residing in Balmoral.

Once the princess can't feel the pea any more, not even when all but one of her mattresses have been whisked away, what is left but a dingy death in a concrete tunnel?

2 August 2007

You have a nice country,
I would like to be your son

Bee Wilson

ASKED IN AN EXAM at the age of 16 whether kings should be elected, the future Edward VII answered: 'It is better than hereditary
right because you have more chance of having a good sovereign,
if it goes by hereditary right if you have a bad or weak sovereign,
you cannot prevent him reigning.' By Bertie's feeble standards,
this was a flash of insight. For the 59 years that he was prince
of Wales, his mother despaired of him. In 1863, she wailed in a
letter to her daughter Alice that Bertie – now 21 – 'shows more
and more how totally, totally unfit he is for ever becoming King!'
Neither Victoria nor the constitution could prevent him from
ascending to the throne on her death. It didn't matter. Bertie –
this generally amiable but foolish and corpulent cigar-smoking,
tiger-shooting adulterer – was a perfectly respectable king. All he
had to do was be himself and his people adored him. In the end,
like his mother, he gave his name to an age.

Jane Ridley's absorbing new biography shows that Victoria
was horrified by her eldest son almost from the moment he was
born.* As a baby, he looked 'too frightful' and was 'sadly back-
ward'. The queen compared him unfavourably with his older sister Vicky, who was far cleverer, spoke French at the age of three
and read Shakespeare and Gibbon for fun. But the unfailing

---

* *Bertie: A Life of Edward VII* (Chatto, 2012).

point of comparison was her sainted Albert, against whom Bertie never had any chance of measuring up. She named him Albert Edward, but when he was 18 months wrote: 'I do not think him worthy of being called Albert yet.' She was anxious to prevent the boy from taking precedence over her husband and bestowed the title of prince consort on Albert to give him a rank above prince of Wales, while also making sure Bertie's name came after Albert's in the nation's prayers.

The education Bertie received from his parents was monstrously harsh and unsurprisingly it neither reined him in nor sharpened him up. At two and a half, a phrenologist examined the bumps on his head and diagnosed 'defective' brain development. At four, another doctor found the child 'nervous and excitable with little power of sustained action in any direction'. His governess, Lady Lyttelton, lamented his 'passions and stampings' and inclination to hurl his books and sit under the table. Victoria and Albert's solution was a heavily timetabled regime, modelled on Albert's own German education. From the age of six, every half-hour of Bertie's day was accounted for, from eight in the morning to six at night. At seven, he was taken out of the nursery and given a still more brutal routine, seeing no one except his tutors all day, apart from 15 minutes spent with his parents in the morning and evening. If all this was intended to make him more of an Albert and less of a Bertie, it failed. His tutors found him excitable, with dreadfully weak powers of concentration. Once more, Prince Albert consulted a phrenologist. Again, the news was bad. Bertie's anterior lobe, supposedly responsible for intellect, was said to be small. 'I wonder whence that Anglo-Saxon brain of his has come,' Albert said. 'It must have descended from the Stuarts, for the family have been purely German since their day.'

To those outside the family, Bertie seemed all too German. He rolled his rs in the German fashion all his life. Violet Trefusis, the daughter of his last great mistress, Alice Keppel, remembered a kind man with a 'rich German accent' who 'smelled deliciously of cigars and eau de Portugal'. Ridley suggests that 'his fluency in German' may have been one of the factors slowing down his learning since it 'interfered with his speaking of English'. Yet his parents worried that the boy wasn't German enough. His marriage – an arranged union with the waif-like Princess Alexandra of Denmark – caused the queen renewed anguish, even though she had been the one to engineer it. First, there was the question of Alix's tiny skull. 'Are you aware,' Victoria wrote to Vicky, 'that Alix has the smallest head ever seen?' The fear was that with Alix's small head and Bertie's inadequate brain, 'future children' would be brainless. The greater fear was that they would be too Danish. 'A Danish partisan you must never be,' she lectured Bertie, 'or you put yourself against your whole family and against your Mother and Sovereign – who (God knows!) has been as impartial as anyone ever was!' At the height of the Schleswig-Holstein crisis of 1864 – the dispute was between Denmark, Austria and Prussia – Victoria reminded Bertie that 'your whole family are German and you are yourself half German.'

This was something clever Vicky, who had cleverly married Fritz of Prussia, never needed to be reminded of. Bertie, by contrast, seems to have had mixed feelings about being German even before his marriage. As a child, he showed signs of being drawn to the old enemy, France. One of his best childhood experiences was a ten-day state visit to France in August 1855 with his parents and Vicky. They were the guests of Napoleon III, who drove Bertie round Paris in a curricle. Wearing Highland dress, Bertie knelt at Napoleon's tomb as the band played 'God Save the Queen' and the French crowd went wild, just as they would go wild for him in 1903, when he visited Paris as king, the greatest triumph of his monarchy. The 14-year-old Bertie turned to Napoleon III and remarked: 'You have a nice country, I would like to be your son.'

You can see why the boy might have liked this lush French womaniser for a father instead of cold, German Albert. The prince consort 'spied on Bertie', Ridley writes, 'he whipped him, he treated him as a patient. He never tried to engage his sympathy or initiate him into the world of English manhood.' When Florence Nightingale met the boy she found him 'a little cowed, as if he had been overtaught'. Others found him either rude and rebellious or pathetically childish. The only tutor to develop any emotional bond with Bertie, a handsome former Eton master called Henry Birch, was sacked by Albert for not being Presbyterian enough and for himself being found to have an unsatisfactory skull when the phrenologist was called to examine it. Albert kept setting Bertie tasks at which he couldn't fail to disappoint. When he was 15, he was made to attend Faraday's Christmas Lectures on Attraction at the Royal Institution and produce reports on what he had learned. But the neatly written copperplate pages amounted to no more than 'an inaccurate stringing together of the notes!' Albert lamented. When Bertie spent a year at Trinity College, Cambridge in 1861, Albert upped the ante, forbidding him from taking any notes at lectures, forcing him to reproduce what he had learned from memory when he returned to his large draughty residence at Madingley Hall.

The same year, Albert opened a dossier entitled 'Bertie's Marriage Prospects'. Princess Alexandra was the lead candidate from the start: she was pretty and had been 'very strictly kept' according to Vicky, who noted approvingly that she had not 'read a novel of any kind'. 'From that photograph I would marry her at once,' Albert creepily remarked when shown a picture of Alexandra at 16. But Victoria feared that Bertie's hopeless Bertieness would get in the way. Her son was 'sallow, dull, blasé'; how was he to make himself 'worthy' of this 'jewel'? Victoria, Albert and Vicky had discussed the matter in some detail before they thought to include Bertie, or even to inform him of the existence of this 'Danish pearl'. When Bertie got cold feet, Albert angrily told him he was duty-bound to propose. The hope was that marriage might finally correct the weakness the tutors had failed to deal with.

Given this upbringing, the question was not whether Bertie would rebel, but how. Soon after his exciting trip to Paris, he and his 11-year-old brother Affie were caught smoking in secret. But that outlet for rebellion was taken away on his 19th birthday when Albert officially granted him permission to smoke. The one means of escape that remained – it would always be Bertie's greatest weakness – was sex. Bertie took his first mistress while his parents were negotiating his marriage. Nellie Clifden was a serial army girlfriend, whom his friend Charles Carrington referred to as 'a well known "London Lady" much run after by the Household Brigade'. She seduced Bertie while he was attending a military camp at the Curragh in Ireland. We know exactly when he first made love to her – and the second and third occasions – because he recorded it in an engagement diary:

6 Sept Curragh N.C. – 1st time
9 Sept Curragh N.C. – 2nd time
10 Sept Curragh N.C. – 3rd time

Despite the brilliant cunning of what Ridley calls 'these cryptic notes' – who would have guessed that 'N.C.' stood for Nellie Clifden? – Bertie was found out. Rumours started to circulate that he had smuggled Nellie into Windsor Castle for his 20th birthday on 9 November 1861. Three days later, the rumours reached his father's ears. Albert did not react well.

The prince consort was still only 42, but he was old in looks, temperament and health. He was 'paunchy' and bald, Ridley writes, and 'always cold' – 'when he rose early to work on dark winter mornings, he wore a wig to warm his bald pate.' The news that Bertie had 'fallen' provoked a long letter from Albert claiming that it had caused him 'the deepest pain I have yet felt in this life'. Were Bertie to lose the Danish pearl, he wrote, 'the consequences for this country & for the world at large would be too dreadful.' Why, oh why, he asked, 'did you not open yourself to your father' at the point of temptation? If only Bertie had confided in Albert when he was experiencing these 'sexual passions', his father would have reminded him of 'the special mode in which these desires are to be gratified' – 'the holy ties of Matrimony'. Which may explain why Bertie didn't consult his father about his plan to sleep with a well-known army hooker.

Bertie did his best to apologise. He insisted, truthfully, that Nellie wasn't at Windsor on the night of his birthday. He didn't mention that a different prostitute was there. He grovelled. On 25 November, Albert came to visit him in Cambridge, so that they could have it out again. They stayed up talking on a wet and stormy night until one in the morning. According to his wife, Albert forgave Bertie for his 'fall', which is more than she ever did. When Albert died of pneumonia a couple of weeks later, the queen over and over again blamed Bertie for making his father ill with worry. It is now thought that Albert may have suffered from Crohn's disease, a progressive inflammation of the gut. But for Victoria, Albert's lowness of mind and body had clearly been brought on by Bertie's behaviour. 'Oh! That boy ... I never can or shall look at him without a shudder.'

The extraordinary thing is that before he could become king Bertie still had another forty years in which to play the errant, dissolute prince of Wales, forty more years in which to carry on disappointing his mother. Albert was wrong about Bertie's fall destroying his chance of marrying Alix of Denmark. Alix told one of his sisters that she would have married him just as happily had he been a 'cowboy' not a prince, which was lucky because in a way he was. The wedding took place in the spring of 1863. The day before it, Victoria took the couple to visit Albert in the mausoleum at Frogmore, so that the corpse could give his blessing – a 'very touching moment', according to Victoria. The tiny-waisted bride wore Honiton lace and orange blossom. For decades, she was the most celebrated fashion plate in the country. Children ensued: Eddy, Georgie, Maud, Victoria and Louise. Their heads were not alarmingly small. There was huge sadness when 'slow and dawdly' Eddy, the heir, died of influenza at the age of 28. His fiancée, May of Teck, married his younger brother Georgie, who would reign as George V after his father's death. And so Albert's line continued.

Bertie didn't mend his ways; but contrary to Albert's fears, the consequences for world politics weren't too dreadful. Walter Bagehot wrote in *The English Constitution* that 'all the world and all the glory of it, whatever is most attractive, whatever is most seductive, has always been offered to the prince of Wales of the day and always will be.' In his appetite for claiming the pleasures of the world, Bertie was the archetypal prince of Wales. There were many mistresses besides Lillie Langtry and Alice Keppel, the really famous ones. To be Bertie's mistress, it seems you needed a large bosom and a soothing manner, and the patience to endure endless 'boresome' hours on the sofa while he goggled at you, as Daisy Warwick, one of his longest-standing mistresses, put it. He called her his little 'Daisywife' and fed her suppers of lobster and champagne. When they had an assignation, he carefully noted 'D' in his diary, just as he had with Nellie all those years before. Daisy complained that he monopolised her leisure. 'In 1893,' Ridley writes, '"D" is written on an astonishing 69 days, sometimes twice or even three times a day.'

Bertie had time on his hands. Despite being a largely absent monarch after Albert's death, Victoria was adamant that Bertie must not be trusted with too many royal responsibilities. So he filled his weeks and years with women, dancing, horse racing, playing cards, taking rest cures at Marienbad and shooting – he recorded 8463 pheasants over four days at one Leicestershire house party. And guzzling:

> Shooting breakfast typically consisted of poulet sauté aux champignons, rump steaks pommes, saucisson doré and oeufs brouillés aux truffes. Shooting lunch was: Don Pedro sherry, curry of rabbits, ronde de boeuf, partridges, roast beef, galantine foie gras, wild boar, apple pudding and rum baba.

At Sandringham near the Norfolk coast, Bertie would swallow 'several dozen oysters in minutes'. The house parties, as described by Ridley, both those he gave and those to which he was invited, were stupendous. By the end, though, despite the honour of having Bertie cross your threshold, the invitations started to dry up. 'The cost of entertaining him – estimated at anything from £5000 to £10,000 per house party – was becoming prohibitive.' (That's up to half a million in today's money.)

FOR A MAN of his world and upbringing, some of Bertie's views were surprising. Though he drank champagne in great volume, he hated drunkenness. At one shooting party at Sandringham, he admonished Sir Frederick Johnstone: 'Freddy, Freddy, you're very drunk.' Johnstone unwisely replied, imitating Bertie's German rs: 'Tum Tum, you're verrry fat!' Johnstone was forced to leave Sandringham before breakfast the next day. Another of Bertie's bugbears was the racism of the Raj. He thoroughly enjoyed shooting tigers in India, boasting to his nine-year-old son Georgie that he had shot six in one day and 'some were very savage – two were "man eaters".' But he diverged from his imperial hosts on their free use of the word 'nigger', complaining to Lord Glanville that 'because a man has a black face and a different religion from our own, there is no reason why he should be treated as a brute.' This was a rare question on which he and his mother saw eye to eye. She too found it 'dreadful how they treat these poor creatures'.

Bertie was unusual, too, in his denouncing of anti-semitism and fondness for Jewish friends, if they were rich enough. He complained to the journalist W.T. Stead about the persecution of the Jews in Russia. The archdukes of Austria 'gasped' when he accepted the hospitality of Baron Maurice Hirsch, a Jewish-Austrian financier. Daisy Warwick admitted that the rest of the prince's crowd 'resented the introduction of Jews into the social set ... not because we disliked them ... but because they had brains and understood finance. As a class, we did not like brains.' On this front, Bertie fitted in just fine. He never read a book if he could avoid it. Shortly before his coronation, he needed an operation to lance an abscess, brought on by gorging on hard lobster. While convalescing, Ridley writes, 'he read novels, a sure sign that he was ill. He thought them all very poor, especially Conan Doyle's *Hound of the Baskervilles*.' After his mother's death, he told the Windsor librarian to pack up Albert's carefully assembled collection of books and 'get rid of those which were not required'.

After forty years of waiting, Bertie finally took the crown in 1901. It is the thesis of Ridley's wonderfully amusing book that he proved himself in the end to be like 'Shakespeare's Prince Hal, the dissolute prince who reformed after his accession to become the modern king'. This is going too far. Prince Hal was 16 when he fought Harry Hotspur at Shrewsbury in 1403 and only 26 when he became king. For Bertie, by contrast, the womanising and games were not youthful indiscretions but an entrenched way of life. He was nearly fifty when he was implicated in the Tranby Croft scandal, a legal skirmish over a game of baccarat. Nor did kingship curb his appetites. Alice Keppel's daughters Sonia and Violet remembered Mama taking long drives with the man they called 'Kingy' from the Hotel du Palais in Biarritz. Sometimes, he let the children play a game where they put two pieces of buttered bread on his trouser leg to see which fell faster.

The main claim for King Edward VII's reputation rests, as Ridley notes, 'upon his role in foreign policy'. His most notable achievement in that field was his trip to Paris in May 1903: it helped lay the ground for the Anglo-French Entente of 1904, which defused the danger of war with France (though it did nothing to stop the eventual war with Germany). He gave charming speeches in fluent French; the English press hailed his triumph. Ridley complains that the politicians subsequently wrote him out of history, saying of Balfour's insistence that the king had 'nothing to do' with the entente: 'What Balfour failed to acknowledge was that the king's visit to Paris was policy in itself.'

This is to set the bar pretty low for what was required of a British monarch by 1903. If being a smiling, waving celebrity was enough, Bertie was brilliant at being king; but it was not exactly the role Henry V assumed on the death of his father. 'There is something comic in the great British nation with its infinite variety of talents, having this undistinguished and limited-minded German bourgeois to be its social sovereign,' Beatrice Webb noted as she watched him dole out prizes to London schoolchildren four years before he became king. Henry James was equally unimpressed by the accession of this 'arch-vulgarian'. But Bertie turned out to be very good at the rigmarole and regalia of monarchy. Despite his louche private life, he was a stickler for protocol and correct dress when it came to public appearances. Even his grandchildren had to remember to kiss him on the hand before kissing him on the cheek. Though generally indolent and greedy, he could be hard-working when the work was ceremonial. On one day alone, he bestowed three thousand Boer War medals. He showered decorations 'like confetti', Ridley writes. 'He subscribes to his cripples, rewards his sailors, reviews his soldiers and opens bridges, bazaars, hospitals and railway tunnels with enviable sweetness,' Asquith's wife observed. Victoria and Albert despaired for their poor strange boy with his poor strange brain because they believed that the character and talents of the monarch were of critical importance for the nation.

Is it better for a king to be elected or hereditary? What Bertie could have said is that the answer depends on the weight kingship holds. If being king was a job Bertie was good at, it can't have been much of a job. Ridley argues that Edward VII was the first British monarch to come to terms with what it meant to be a constitutional monarch:

> He did not debate policy with his ministers; he showed no party preferences, nor did he veto ministerial appointments. But this did not mean that he was a weak king. He relinquished the powers of the Crown, but he greatly expanded its influence.

Bertie's influence, however, was not the influence of politics but of celebrity. He 'adored being king' and adored thinking of himself as having a people. He was enraged when taken to task for inquiring after the health of the republican Keir Hardie: 'I am King of ALL the People!' he bellowed. They, in turn, doted on him. It is estimated that 400,000 people came to pay their respects at Westminster Abbey after he died – far bigger crowds than turned out for Victoria.

27 September 2012

Royal Bodies

Hilary Mantel

LAST SUMMER at the festival in Hay-on-Wye, I was asked to name a famous person and choose a book to give them. I hate the leaden repetitiveness of these little quizzes: who would be the guests at your ideal dinner party, what book has changed your life, which fictional character do you most resemble? I had to come up with an answer, however, so I chose Kate, the Duchess of Cambridge, and I chose to give her a book published in 2006, by the cultural historian Caroline Weber; it's called *Queen of Fashion: What Marie Antoinette Wore to the Revolution*. It's not that I think we're heading for a revolution. It's rather that I saw Kate becoming a jointed doll on which certain rags are hung. In those days she was a shop-window mannequin, with no personality of her own, entirely defined by what she wore. These days she is a mother-to-be, and draped in another set of threadbare attributions. Once she gets over being sick, the press will find that she is radiant. They will find that this young woman's life until now was nothing, her only point and purpose being to give birth.

Marie Antoinette was a woman eaten alive by her frocks. She was transfixed by appearances, stigmatised by her fashion choices. Politics were made personal in her. Her greed for self-gratification, her half-educated dabbling in public affairs, were adduced as a reason the French were bankrupt and miserable. It was ridiculous, of course. She was one individual with limited power and influence, who focused the rays of misogyny. She was a woman who couldn't win. If she wore fine fabrics she was said to be extravagant. If she wore simple fabrics, she was accused of plotting to ruin the Lyon silk trade. But in truth she was all body and no soul: no soul, no sense, no sensitivity. She was so wedded to her appearance that when the royal family, in disguise, made its desperate escape from Paris, dashing for the border, she not only had several trunk loads of new clothes sent on in advance, but took her hairdresser along on the trip. Despite the weight of her mountainous hairdos, she didn't feel her head wobbling on her shoulders. When she returned from that trip, to the prison Paris would become for her, it was said that her hair had turned grey overnight.

Antoinette as a royal consort was a gliding, smiling disaster, much like Diana in another time and another country. But Kate Middleton, as she was, appeared to have been designed by a committee and built by craftsmen, with a perfect plastic smile and the spindles of her limbs hand-turned and gloss-varnished. When it was announced that Diana was to join the royal family, the Duke of Edinburgh is said to have given her his approval because she would 'breed in some height'. Presumably Kate was designed to breed in some manners. She looks like a nicely brought up young lady, with 'please' and 'thank you' part of her vocabulary. But in her first official portrait by Paul Emsley, unveiled in January, her eyes are dead and she wears the strained smile of a woman who really wants to tell the painter to bugger off. One critic said perceptively that she appeared 'weary of being looked at'. Another that the portrait might pass muster as the cover of a Catherine Cookson novel: an opinion I find thought-provoking, as Cookson's simple tales of poor women extricating themselves from adverse circumstances were for twenty years, according to the Public Lending Right statistics, the nation's favourite reading. Sue Townsend said of Diana that she was 'a fatal non-reader'. She didn't know the end of her own story. She enjoyed only the romances of Barbara Cartland. I'm far too snobbish to have read one, but I assume they are stories in which a wedding takes place and they all live happily ever after. Diana didn't see the possible twists in the narrative. What does Kate read? It's a question.

Kate seems to have been selected for her role of princess because she was irreproachable: as painfully thin as anyone could wish, without quirks, without oddities, without the risk of the emergence of character. She appears precision-made, machine-made, so different from Diana whose human awkwardness and emotional incontinence showed in her every gesture. Diana was capable of transforming herself from galumphing schoolgirl to ice queen, from wraith to Amazon. Kate seems capable of going from perfect bride to perfect mother, with no messy deviation. When her pregnancy became public she had been visiting her old school, and had picked up a hockey stick and run a few paces for the camera. BBC News devoted a discussion to whether a pregnant woman could safely put on a turn of speed while wearing high heels. It is sad to think that intelligent people could devote themselves to this topic with earnest furrowings of the brow, but that's what discourse about royals comes to: a compulsion to comment, a discourse empty of content, mouthed rather than spoken. And in the same way one is compelled to look at them: to ask what they are made of, and is their substance the same as ours.

I used to think that the interesting issue was whether we should have a monarchy or not. But now I think that question is rather like, should we have pandas or not? Our current royal family doesn't have the difficulties in breeding that pandas do, but pandas and royal persons alike are expensive to conserve and ill-adapted to any modern environment. But aren't they interesting? Aren't they nice to look at? Some people find them endearing; some pity them for their precarious situation; everybody stares at them, and however airy the enclosure they inhabit, it's still a cage.

A few years ago I saw the Prince of Wales at a public award

ceremony. I had never seen him before, and at once I thought: what a beautiful suit! What sublime tailoring! It's for Shakespeare to penetrate the heart of a prince, and for me to study his cuff buttons. I found it hard to see the man inside the clothes; and like Thomas Cromwell in my novels, I couldn't help winding the fabric back onto the bolt and pricing him by the yard. At this ceremony, which was formal and carefully orchestrated, the prince gave an award to a young author who came up on stage in shirtsleeves to receive his cheque. He no doubt wished to show that he was a free spirit, despite taking money from the establishment. For a moment I was ashamed of my trade. I thought, this is what the royals have to contend with today: not real, principled opposition, but self-congratulatory chippiness.

And then as we drifted away from the stage I saw something else. I glanced sideways into a room off the main hall, and saw that it was full of stacking chairs. It was a depressing, institutional, impersonal sight. I thought, Charles must see this all the time. Glance sideways, into the wings, and you see the tacky preparations for the triumphant public event. You see your beautiful suit deconstructed, the tailor's chalk lines, the unsecured seams. You see that your life is a charade, that the scenery is cardboard, that the paint is peeling, the red carpet fraying, and if you linger you will notice the oily devotion fade from the faces of your subjects, and you will see their retreating backs as they turn up their collars and button their coats and walk away into real life.

Then a little later I went to Buckingham Palace for a book trade event, a large evening party. I had expected to see people pushing themselves into the queen's path, but the opposite was true. The queen walked through the reception areas at an even pace, hoping to meet someone, and you would see a set of guests, as if swept by the tide, parting before her or welling ahead of her into the next room. They acted as if they feared excruciating embarrassment should they be caught and obliged to converse.

The self-possessed became gauche and the eloquent were struck dumb. The guests studied the walls, the floor, they looked everywhere except at Her Majesty. They studied exhibits in glass cases and the paintings on the walls, which were of course worth looking at, but they studied them with great intentness, as if their eyes had been glued. Vermeer was just then 'having a moment', as they say, and the guests congregated around a small example, huddled with their backs to the room. I pushed through to see the painting along with the others but I can't remember now which Vermeer it was. It's safe to say there would have been a luminous face, round or oval, there would have been a woman gazing entranced at some household object, or perhaps reading a letter with a half-smile; there may have been a curtain, suggestive of veiled meaning; there would have been an enigma. We concentrated on it at the expense of the enigma moving among us, smiling with gallant determination.

And then the queen passed close to me and I stared at her. I am ashamed now to say it but I passed my eyes over her as a cannibal views his dinner, my gaze sharp enough to pick the meat off her bones. I felt that such was the force of my devouring curiosity that the party had dematerialised and the walls melted and there were only two of us in the vast room, and such was the hard power of my stare that Her Majesty turned and looked back at me, as if she had been jabbed in the shoulder; and for a split second her face expressed not anger but hurt bewilderment. She looked young: for a moment she had turned back from a figurehead into the young woman she was, before monarchy froze her and made her a thing, a thing which only had meaning when it was exposed, a thing that existed only to be looked at.

And I felt sorry then. I wanted to apologise. I wanted to say: it's nothing personal, it's monarchy I'm staring at. I rejoined, mentally, the rest of the guests. Now flunkeys were moving among us with trays and on them were canapés, and these snacks were the queen's revenge. They were pieces of gristly meat on skewers. Let's not put too fine a point on it: they were kebabs. It took some time to chew through one of them, and then the guests were left with the little sticks in their hands. They tried to give them back to the flunkeys, but the flunkeys smiled and sadly shook their heads, and moved away, so the guests had to carry on the evening holding them out, like children with sparklers on Guy Fawkes night.

We can be sure the queen was not traumatised by my staring, as when next we met she gave me a medal. As I prepared to go to the palace, people would say: 'Will it be the actual queen, the queen herself?' Did they think contact with the anointed hand would change you? Was that what the guests at the palace feared: to be changed by powerful royal magic, without knowing how? The faculty of awe remains intact, for all that the royal story in recent years has taken a sordid turn. There were scandals enough in centuries past, from the sneaky little adulteries of Katherine Howard to the junketings of the Prince Regent to the modern-day mischief of Mrs Simpson. But a new world began, I think, in 1980, with the discovery that Diana, the future Princess of Wales, had legs. You will remember how the young Diana taught for a few hours a week at a kindergarten called Young England, and when it was first known that she was Charles's choice of bride, the press photographed her, infants touchingly gathered around; but they induced her to stand against the light, so in the resulting photograph the nation could see straight through her skirt. A sort of licentiousness took hold, a national lip-smacking. Those gangling limbs were artlessly exposed, without her permission. It was the first violation.

When Diana drove to St Paul's she was a blur of virginal white behind glass. The public was waiting to see the dress, but this was more than a fashion moment. An everyday sort of girl had been squashed into the coach, but a goddess came out. She didn't get out of the coach in any ordinary way: she hatched. The extraordinary dress came first, like a flow of liquid, like ectoplasm emerging from the orifices of a medium. It was a long moment before she solidified. Indeed the coach was a medium, a method of conveyance and communication between two spheres, the private and the public, the common and the royal. The dress's first effect was dismaying. I could hear a nation of women catching their breath as one, not in awe but in horror: it's creased to glory, how did they let that happen? I heard the squeak as a million ironing-boards unfolded, a sigh and shudder as a collective nightmare came true: that dream we all have, that we are incorrectly dressed or not dressed at all, that we are naked in the street. But as the dress resolved about her, the princess was born and the world breathed out.

Diana was more royal than the family she joined. That had nothing to do with family trees. Something in her personality, her receptivity, her passivity, fitted her to be the carrier of myth. She came near to claiming that she had a healing touch, the ancient attribute of royal persons. The healing touch can't be felt through white gloves. Diana walked bare-handed among the multitude, and unarmed: unfortified by irony, uninformed by history. Her tragedy was located in the gap between her human capacities and the demands of the superhuman role she was required to fulfil. When I think of Diana, I remember Stevie Smith's poem about the Lorelei:

There, on a rock majestical,
A girl with smile equivocal,
Painted, young and damned and fair,
Sits and combs her yellow hair.

Soon Diana's hairstyles were as consequential as Marie Antoinette's, and a great deal cheaper to copy.

In the next stage of her story, she passed through trials, through ordeals at the world's hands. For a time the public refrained from demanding her blood so she shed it herself, cutting her arms and legs. Her death still makes me shudder because although I know it was an accident, it wasn't just an accident. It was fate showing her hand, fate with her twisted grin. Diana visited the most feminine of cities to meet her end as a woman: to move on, from the City of Light to the place beyond black. She went into the underpass to be reborn, but reborn this time without a physical body: the airy subject of a hundred thousand photographs, a flicker at the corner of the eye, a sigh on the breeze.

For a time it was hoped, and it was feared, that Diana had changed the nation. Her funeral was a pagan outpouring, a lawless fiesta of grief. We are bad at mourning our dead. We don't make time or space for grief. The world tugs us along, back into its harsh rhythm before we are ready for it, and for the pain of loss doctors can prescribe a pill. We are at war with our nature, and nature will win; all the bottled anguish, the grief dammed up, burst the barriers of politeness and formality and restraint, and broke down the divide between private and public, so that strangers wailed in the street, people who had never met Diana lamented her with maladjusted fervour, and we all remembered our secret pain and unleashed it in one huge carnival of mass mourning. But in the end, nothing changed. We were soon back to the prosaic: shirtsleeves, stacking chairs, little sticks. And yet none of us who lived through it will forget that dislocating time, when the skin came off the surface of the world, and our inner vision cleared, and we saw the archetypes clear and plain, and we saw the collective psyche at work, and the gods pulling our strings. To quote Stevie Smith again:

An antique story comes to me
And fills me with anxiety,
I wonder why I fear so much
What surely has no modern touch?

In looking at royalty we are always looking at what is archaic, what is mysterious by its nature, and my feeling is that it will only ever half-reveal itself. This poses a challenge to historians and to those of us who work imaginatively with the past. Royal persons are both gods and beasts. They are persons but they are supra-personal, carriers of a blood line: at the most basic, they are breeding stock, collections of organs.

THIS BRINGS ME to the royal bodies with whom I have been most concerned recently, those of Anne Boleyn and Henry VIII. Long before Kate's big news was announced, the tabloids wanted to look inside her to see if she was pregnant. Historians are still trying to peer inside the Tudors. Are they healthy, are they sick, can they breed? The story of Henry and his wives is peculiar to its time and place, but also timeless and universally understood; it is highly political and also highly personal. It is about body parts, about what slots in where, and when: are they body parts fit for purpose, or are they diseased? It's no surprise that so much fiction constellates around the subject of Henry and his wives. Often, if you want to write about women in history, you have to distort history to do it, or substitute fantasy for facts; you have to pretend that individual women were more important than they were or that we know more about them than we do.

But with the reign of King Bluebeard, you don't have to pretend. Women, their bodies, their reproductive capacities, their animal nature, are central to the story. The history of the reign is so graphically gynaecological that in the past it enabled lady novelists to write about sex when they were only supposed to write about love; and readers could take an avid interest in what went on in royal bedrooms by dignifying it as history, therefore instructive, edifying. Popular fiction about the Tudors has also been a form of moral teaching about women's lives, though what is taught varies with moral fashion. It used to be that Anne

Boleyn was a man-stealer who got paid out. Often, now, the lesson is that if Katherine of Aragon had been a bit more foxy, she could have hung on to her husband. Anne as opportunist and sexual predator finds herself recruited to the cause of feminism. Always, the writers point to the fact that a man who marries his mistress creates a job vacancy. 'Women beware women' is a teaching that never falls out of fashion.

Anne Boleyn, in particular, is a figure who elicits a deep response, born out of ignorance often enough but also out of empathy. The internet is abuzz with stories about her, as if everything were happening today. Her real self is hidden within the dramas into which we co-opt her. There is a prurient curiosity around her, of the kind that gathered around Wallis Simpson. Henry didn't give up the throne to marry her, but he did reshape his nation's history. So what was her particular attraction? Did she have a sexual secret? A special trick? Was she beautiful, or ugly? The six fingers with which she was credited were not seen during her lifetime, and the warts and wens and extra nipple that supposedly disfigured her were witches' marks produced by the black fantasy of Catholic propagandists. Her contemporaries didn't think she was a great beauty. 'She is of middling stature,' a Venetian diplomat reported. A 'swarthy complexion, long neck, wide mouth, bosom not much raised, and in fact has nothing but the English king's great appetite, and her eyes, which are black and beautiful'. It was said, though not by unbiased observers, that after her marriage she aged rapidly and grew thin. If this is true, and we put it together with reports of a swelling in her throat, and with the description of her by one contemporary as 'a goggle-eyed whore', then we're looking, possibly, at a woman with a hyperthyroid condition, a woman of frayed temper who lives on the end of her nerves. It often surprises people that there is no attested contemporary portrait. Just because an unknown hand has written 'Anne Boleyn' on a picture, it doesn't mean it's an image from the life or even an image of Anne at all. The most familiar image, in which she wears a letter 'B' hanging from a pearl necklace, exists in many forms and variants and originates at least fifty years after Anne's death.

So much close scrutiny, and none of it much help to posterity. Anne was a mercurial woman, still shaped by the projections of those who read and write about her. Royal bodies do change after death, and not just as a consequence of the universal post-mortem changes. Now we know the body in the Leicester car park is indeed that of Richard III, we have to concede the curved spine was not Tudor propaganda, but we need not believe the chronicler who claimed Richard was the product of a two-year pregnancy and was born with teeth. Why are we all so pleased about digging up a king? Perhaps because the present is paying some of the debt it owes to the past, and science has come to the aid of history. The king stripped by the victors has been reclothed in his true identity. This is the essential process of history, neatly illustrated: loss, retrieval.

To return to Henry VIII: almost the first thirty years of his reign were shaped by his need for a male heir. Religious and political activity cluster around the subject. Not all the intelligence and diligence of his ministers could give Henry what he most needed. Only a woman could: but which woman? Neither of Henry's first two wives had trouble conceiving. Royal pregnancies were not announced in those days; the news generally crept out, and public anticipation was aroused only when the child quickened. We know Katherine of Aragon had at least six pregnancies, most of them ending in late miscarriages or neonatal deaths. She had a son who survived for seven weeks, but only one child made it past early infancy, and that was a daughter, the Princess Mary. Anne's first pregnancy was successful, and produced another girl, the Princess Elizabeth. Then she miscarried at least twice. It was not until his third marriage that Henry had a son who lived.

Both those daughters, Mary and Elizabeth, were women of great ability, and in their very different ways were capable of ruling; but I don't think this means that Henry was wrong in his construction of his situation. What he feared was that his bloodline would end. Elizabeth found the puzzle of whom she could marry too difficult to solve, so that her reign was dominated by succession crises, and she was indeed the last of the Tudors. The line did end: just a lot later than Henry had imagined.

Anne Boleyn wasn't royal by birth. Her family were city merchants dignified into gentlefolk, and her father had married into the powerful and noble Howard family. She became royal, exalted, at her coronation when, six months pregnant, she walked the length of Westminster Abbey on a cloth of heaven-blue. It was said she had won Henry by promising him a son. Anne was a power player, a clever and determined woman. But in the end she was valued for her body parts, not her intellect or her soul; it was her womb that was central to her story. The question is whether she could ever win the battle for an heir: or was biology against her? At his trial Anne's brother, George Boleyn, entertained the court by telling them that Henry was no good in bed. Conception was thought to be tied to female orgasm, so the implication was that what George called Henry's lack of 'skill' was the problem.

Yet clearly he was able to make his wives pregnant. Was something else wrong? The old notion that Henry had syphilis has been discarded. There never was any contemporary evidence for it. The theory was constructed in the 19th century, as part of a narrative that showed Henry as a sexual beast justly punished for his promiscuity. In fact Henry constrained his sexual appetites. He had few mistresses compared to other grandees of his time. I think it was more important to him to be good, to be seen to be good, than to be gratified in this particular way. In fact I think we can say that the old monster was a bit of a romantic. Later in life, when he married Anne of Cleves, he didn't want to have sex with a woman with whom he wasn't in love; it was a scruple that baffled his contemporaries.

Recently a new hypothesis about Henry has emerged. In 2010 a paper by Catrina Banks Whitley and Kyra Cornelius Kramer appeared in the *Historical Journal*, called 'A New Explanation of the Reproductive Woes and Midlife Decline of Henry VIII'. It suggested that Henry had a blood type called Kells positive. People who are Kells positive carry an extra antibody on the surface of their red blood cells. The blood type is rare, so we can assume Henry's wives were Kells negative, and that their lack of compatibility was the reason for the multiple reproductive failures. When a woman who is Kells negative conceives by a man who is Kells positive, she will, if the foetus itself is Kells positive, become sensitised; her immune system will try to reject the foetus. The first pregnancy will go well, other things being equal. As with rhesus incompatibility, it takes one pregnancy for the woman to develop the sensitisation. But later children will die before or just after birth.

To a certain point this fits Henry's story. He had a healthy illegitimate son by Elizabeth Blount: that was a first pregnancy. His first child with Anne Boleyn was a healthy girl, and his first child with Jane Seymour a healthy boy; Jane died soon after Edward's birth, so we don't know what would have happened thereafter. With Katherine of Aragon the pattern is more blurred. Mystery surrounds her first pregnancy, much of it made by the queen herself, who perhaps didn't want to admit that she had miscarried; so we know the pregnancy didn't work out, but we don't know what happened. One of Katherine's doctors thought it was a twin pregnancy and it may have failed for any number of reasons. So Katherine's healthy child, Mary, was not her first. But every child fathered by Henry had a chance of being Kells negative, and the paper's authors suggest that this is how Mary survived.

If this is true, it makes the history of Henry's reign a different sort of tragedy: not a moral but a biological tragedy, inscribed on the body. The efforts of the wives and the politicians and the churchmen didn't avail because a genetic lottery was in operation. What makes the hypothesis persuasive, to some minds, is Henry's later medical history. Some individuals who are Kells positive go on to develop a collection of symptoms called McLeod syndrome. In early life Henry was, by all contemporary accounts, a creature of great beauty. He excelled in every sport. We wonder, of course, did his opponents let the king win? But Henry was not a fool and though he was susceptible to flattery he didn't need flattery of that simple kind; and besides, in a dangerous pursuit like jousting, where one armoured man on an armoured horse is charging at another headlong, the outcome is difficult to control. I think we can take it that he was a star. He collected a number of injuries that stopped him jousting, and then in middle age became stout, eventually gross. He developed a weakness in his legs, and by the end of his life was virtually immobile. It also seems to some authorities that he underwent personality changes in mid-life. It was said that as a young man he was sweet-natured; though the claim would have had a hollow ring if you were Richard Empson or Edmund Dudley, ministers to his father, whom he executed as soon as he came to the throne. But it's incontrovertible that as Henry aged he became increasingly angry, irrational, wilful and out of control. He fits the picture for McLeod syndrome: progressive muscular weakness and nerve deterioration in the lower body, depression, paranoia, an erosion of personality.

Some historians see the year 1536 as a turning point for Henry, personally and politically: that was the year in which Anne Boleyn was beheaded. Certainly his later years were very sad ones for a man who had been so magnificent and imposing. Pathology is at work, but of what kind? It seems to me that there are more obvious explanations for his poor health and the deterioration of his character, and the authors of the original paper didn't really understand the external pressures on the king later in his reign. Henry had suffered accidents in the tiltyard and one of his legs was permanently ulcerated. He probably had osteomyelitis, an infection in the bone. His leg caused him chronic pain and historians – and, I'm afraid, doctors – underestimate what chronic pain can do to sour the temper and wear away both the personality and the intellect. When we call him paranoid, we must acknowledge he was right to think his enemies were everywhere, though he was increasingly bad at working out who they were.

As for depression, he had a great deal to be depressed about: not just his isolation on the world stage, but his own decay and deterioration. He had magnificent portraits created, and left them as his surrogates to stare down at his courtiers while he retreated into smaller, more intimate spaces. Yet he was quite unable to keep private what was happening to his own body. The royal body exists to be looked at. The world's focus on body parts was most acute and searching in the case of Jane Seymour, Henry's third wife. No one understood what Henry saw in Jane, who was not pretty and not young. The imperial ambassador sneered that 'no doubt she has a very fine *enigme*': which is to say, secret part. We have arrived at the crux of the matter: a royal lady is a royal vagina. Along with the reverence and awe accorded to royal persons goes the conviction that the body of the monarch is public property. We are ready at any moment to rip away the veil of respect, and treat royal persons in an inhuman way, making them not more than us but less than us, not really human at all.

Is monarchy a suitable institution for a grown-up nation? I don't know. I have described how my own sympathies were activated and my simple ideas altered. The debate is not high on our agenda. We are happy to allow monarchy to be an entertainment, in the same way that we license strip joints and lap-dancing clubs. Adulation can swing to persecution, within hours, within the same press report: this is what happened to Prince Harry recently. You can understand that anybody treated this way can be destabilised, and that Harry doesn't know which he is, a person or a prince. Diana was spared, at least, the prospect of growing old under the flashbulbs, a crime for which the media would have made her suffer. It may be that the whole phenomenon of monarchy is irrational, but that doesn't mean that when we look at it we should behave like spectators at Bedlam. Cheerful curiosity can easily become cruelty. It can easily become fatal. We don't cut off the heads of royal ladies these days, but we do sacrifice them, and we did memorably drive one to destruction a scant generation ago. History makes fools of us, makes puppets of us, often enough. But it doesn't have to repeat itself. In the current case, much lies within our control. I'm not asking for censorship. I'm not asking for pious humbug and smarmy reverence. I'm asking us to back off and not be brutes. Get your pink frilly frocks out, zhuzh up your platinum locks. We are all Barbara Cartland now. The pen is in our hands. A happy ending is ours to write.

21 February 2013

Always the Same Dream

Ferdinand Mount

YOU NEED to be over seventy now to remember the awful thrill of the announcement: 'I would like it to be known that I have decided not to marry Group Captain Peter Townsend.' For the older generation, Princess Margaret was the unlucky princess. She was our Diana: capricious, passionate, vindictive, doomed to fall in love with rotters, the breakaway royal who hung out with actors and rogues and who was frozen out by a cold-hearted court, finding contentment only in her hospital work and her two children. Both princesses loved the ballet, too, as though the only real freedom lay in the dance. There was a Princess Margaret Set, just as the Prince Regent had the Carlton House Set, Edward VII had the Marlborough House Set, and Edward VIII had the Fort Belvedere Set: three playboys, only one playgirl.

It is 15 years since she died, and memories of her are not as sharp as they were. Which makes Craig Brown's enterprise not only a marvellous freak of literature but a matchless summoner of our yesterdays.* It is a collage, montage or bricolage of glittery bits culled from two hundred biographies, authorised and unauthorised, written by cashiered gossip columnists and treacherous butlers and chauffeurs, plus odds and ends such as the complete transcript of the princess's *Desert Island Discs* and the catalogue of her jewellery, sold after her death for £9 million.

The effect is like one of those sweeping Klimt portraits, in

---

* *Ma'am Darling: 99 Glimpses of Princess Margaret* (Fourth Estate, 2017).

which the comet trail of colourful fragments leaves a lasting, wistful impression of an era on the skids. The book is extremely funny and extremely sad. As Brown says towards the end of it, 'It is Cinderella in reverse. It is hope dashed, happiness mislaid, life mishandled. Nothing is as thrilling as they said it would be; no one is as amusing, as clever, as attractive or as interesting.'

You feel the sadness all the more not because the princess is such an endearing character but because most of the time she is so ghastly and ghastly in a way that brings out the worst in other people. As time goes by, being ghastly is so much expected of her that it becomes her party piece. She specialises in insulting her hosts' every effort to entertain her. In this regard she isn't snobbish. She is just as rude about the rare 1836 Madeira that Lord Carnarvon pours her – 'exactly like petrol' – as she is about the coronation chicken served her at the opening of some sheltered bungalows in Derbyshire: 'This looks like sick.'

In other respects, her snobbery can reach baroque levels. When her husband nearly sets fire to her dress (on purpose) and says, 'Good thing too, I hate that material,' HRH retorts: 'Material is a word we do not use. We call it stuff.' Other forbidden expressions include 'scrambled eggs' (should be 'buttered eggs') and '*placement*' (should be '*place à table*'). She detested her grandmother, Queen Mary, who had deluged her with presents, and claimed that she suffered from an inferiority complex because she had been born only a serene, not a royal highness.

At first nights, she seldom fails to tell the producer or director how much she loathed the show. To Robert Evans, producer of *Love Story*, at the Royal Command Performance of the film: 'Tony saw *Love Story* in New York. Hated it.' When Dennis Main Wilson says, 'Ma'am, I have the honour to produce a little show called *Till Death Us Do Part*,' she cuts down his faux modesty with: 'Isn't that that frightfully dreary thing in the East End?' At the end of *Carousel* at the National Theatre, Richard Eyre escorts her to the door: 'I'm glad you enjoyed the show.' 'I didn't, I can't bear the piece.'

She was just as rude and inconsiderate in private, late to arrive and even later to leave which meant that nobody else could leave either, because she was a stickler for protocol, despite her pretence of informality. She insisted on chain-smoking through every meal, ashing out on her neighbour's plate or person. Like her father, grandfather and great-grandfather, she was a suicidal smoker. At the sale of her effects, Brown counts no less than 37 cigarette-related gilded gewgaws. Having never been to school, not even sharing with her sister in tutorials on constitutional history from the provost of Eton, she was ignorant on most subjects outside the performing arts, but never hesitated to plonk down her opinions.

Yet throughout her life, the glitterati and literati were gagging to meet her, and despite her rudeness kept on coming back for more. Knowing that she was on the Aga Khan's yacht moored below the windows of the villa in Sardinia where he was staying, Cyril Connolly was desperate to clamber aboard, saying that not to meet the Snowdons was 'like being in the Garden of Eden without seeing God'. Marlon Brando persuaded Kenneth Tynan to ask her to dinner à trois and then was so tongue-tied that he couldn't address a word to her except through Tynan: 'Would you ask the princess what she thinks of ...' Tynan himself wanted to postpone his daughter's birthday party until Princess Margaret was back in town. The TV interviewer Russell Harty on his deathbed had his tracheotomy tube removed, in order to be able to tell Alan Bennett that the princess had asked how he was, twice.

Every celebrity seems to have fantasised about sex with the princess. Eddie Fisher claimed that he had had an affair with her. When her marriage was breaking up, Peter Sellers was besotted with the idea that he would be her next husband, besotted with the idea rather than with her, I think. He even tried to persuade his pet astrologer to discover favourable auguries for the match. John Fowles, typically, fantasised about seducing her and imprisoning her underground, not necessarily in that order. Pablo Picasso claimed that only the princess would be a suitable bride to be the châtelaine of his vast new villa, La Californie. At 5'4", he would have towered over her. He made paper crowns for the vinegary art critic Douglas Cooper and his scarcely less acerbic biographer John Richardson, and taught them how to bow properly for his royal wedding (another example of how artists' jokes are almost as unfunny as musicians').

Brown takes the fantasy a stage further by imagining how married life would have worked out for Pablo and Margaret. This is one of a series of counterfactual episodes spattered through the book: what if she had married Peter Townsend after all, what if she had married Jeremy Thorpe, another improbable contender for her hand, what if she had become queen instead of her sister? These capriccios melt beautifully into the text, because we are immersed in a land of dreams. Being a communist or a homosexual is no barrier here to imagining yourself walking up the aisle of Westminster Abbey with the royal trumpeters at full blast.

With typical puckishness, the novelist A.N. Wilson once asked Princess Margaret whether she, like everyone else, dreamed about the queen. Instead of biting his head off, she answered, rather surprisingly: 'Yes, she said, and it was always the same dream. She dreamed that she was disapproved of, she knew she had done something truly awful, something that transgressed everything that she had been brought up to believe, something which had made the queen angry ... she could not rest until she had heard her sister's voice in waking life.'

Her camp followers – never was that phrase more apt – scarcely waited till she had left the room before they started bitching about her, usually in snobbish terms. The snobbery is equally distributed between left and right. Christopher Isherwood called her 'quite a common little thing'. Richard Eyre said that 'if it weren't for the sharp English upper-class voice, you'd say she looks like a Maltese landlady.' Cecil Beaton described her as vulgar and later as 'a poor midgety brute' who had 'gone to pot ... her complexion now a dirty negligee pink satin'. Only matched by Alan Clark's diary entry: 'fat, ugly, dwarflike, lecherous and revoltingly tastelessly behaved' (from a master of deportment). The emphasis on her small stature was almost universal. It was the cruellest thrust, and one suspects a deliberate one, when her husband (himself no giant) made a TV documentary about midgets, which Margaret gamely described as 'not my cup of tea at all. Bit too near home, I'm afraid.' Yet they all went on angling and wangling. Her presence lured every star in Hollywood to the party Tynan threw for her. At her funeral and memorial service, the camp followers were out in force, scurrying home to their diaries to confide afterwards how awful she had been.

She had been a wilful and mischievous child, unlike her dutiful elder sister. In that notorious book *The Little Princesses*, their nanny Marion Crawford, 'Crawfie', who looked after them for 15 years, described how she would mimic Lilibet's methodical preparations for going to bed. Crawfie was never forgiven for the book. There was no royal wreath at her funeral. Margaret said simply: 'she sneaked.'

Whatever she was like to start with, it is clear, I think, that she went downhill after she was not allowed to marry Townsend. It was a hammer blow to her morale. It was also the most interesting thing to happen to the royal family between the abdication and the death of Diana. It soured her for good. It also left the nation in a state of suspended moral animation for years. The affair was an episode in the history not only of divorce but also of deference and authority. Social historians neglect it at their peril. David Kynaston in *Family Britain 1951-57* gives a pretty full account, but in Peter Hennessy's *Having It So Good: Britain in the 1950s* the only Peter Townsend in the index is the sociologist of that name. Even Brown does not quite do justice to the ramifications.

Townsend was the most genuine of war heroes. Born in 1914, he had joined the RAF at the age of 19 and helped to shoot down the first Heinkel to crash on British soil. He claimed two more Heinkels that spring of 1940 and was awarded a DFC. He got a bar to his DFC for shooting down four more aircraft and was himself shot down three times. He was also extremely good-looking.

That much we probably knew, more or less. What may come as a surprise is that he had been appointed equerry to King George as early as 1944, when Margaret was only 14. By then, he had a wife, Rosemary, and a small son. Margaret said, much later, that she really fell in love with him in 1947 when he accompanied the royal family on their tour of South Africa and they rode across the veld together. He himself claimed to have noticed the first spark between them at a picnic at Balmoral in August 1951. At all events, they had known each other for nine years by the time she was spotted picking fluff from his lapel on Coronation Day, 2 June 1953. The version in Townsend's memoir is that it was only after his divorce from Rosemary in December 1952 that their love had been allowed to blossom. Brown is forgivably sceptical: 'Had this impetuous young woman really managed to hide her feelings for a full five and a half years? And had the group captain somehow exercised a similar restraint?'

In a footnote, Brown adds a recollection from the princess's chauffeur, John Larkin, who asked her whether she wanted to keep the same number plate when she replaced her old Rolls-Royce with a newer model. 'No,' she said, ' it refers to something in my past best forgotten.' The number was PM6450, which Larkin interpreted as 'Princess Margaret 6 April 1950'. Could this be the day she lost her virginity? If so, a sporting flourish, to say the least. Brown does not mention the persistent report that Rosemary was aggrieved at having to play the guilty party in order to save the reputation of the royal family, though she did marry her own lover a few months after the divorce.

On learning of the affair, Sir Alan 'Tommy' Lascelles, private secretary to the new queen, told Townsend: 'you must be either mad or bad.' Within a month, he had persuaded Churchill to exile Townsend to Brussels as air attaché, without even giving him time to say goodbye. I once met Lascelles when I was at school, and was startled by his explosion of venom against the Duke of Windsor, whose private secretary he had been before the war. He was memorably unpleasant. The hope was that the separation would cool their love. But on his return two years later, Townsend said that 'our feelings for one another had not changed.' By now, Margaret was 25, and was free under the Royal Marriages Act to marry without the queen's consent. It was time for the establishment to bring up the big guns. On 1 October 1955, Anthony Eden informed the princess that the cabinet had agreed that if she went ahead with the marriage, she would have to renounce her royal rights and her income from the Civil List. In deploying this threat, the government could scarcely be said to be responding to popular hostility to the match. Gallup found that 59 per cent approved of it and only 17 per cent disapproved. So was it the Church of England's influence? Archbishop Geoffrey Fisher, a famous thrasher in his days as headmaster of Repton, was interviewed on TV by Richard Dimbleby on 2 November, two days after the announcement that the marriage would not happen. Fisher maintained that the decision had been the princess's alone and that 'there was no pressure from Church or State.' This was a barefaced lie. We have seen the blunt financial threat from Eden. True, on her meeting with Fisher on 27 October, the princess did indeed say that she had come not to seek his guidance but to tell him of her decision. But at an earlier dinner with him, on 19 October, he had earnestly counselled her to call it off. There was also an extraordinary leader in the *Times* on 26 October, which has all the portentous fingerprints of the editor, Sir William Haley.

According to the *Times*, the queen had 'come to be the symbol of every side of the life of this society, its universal representative in whom her people see their better selves ideally reflected'. That better self had to be reflected in the queen's family. If the marriage went ahead, 'the princess will be entering into a union which vast numbers of her sister's people, all sincerely anxious for her lifelong happiness, cannot in conscience regard as a marriage.' Vast numbers? All evidence suggests that public opinion was overwhelmingly tolerant of the match. When three of the queen's four children got divorced a generation later, there was no suggestion that any of them would have to renounce their titles or emoluments, as Haley urged that Margaret should do. But Haley was not finished. 'That devout men have argued that it is a wrong interpretation of Christianity is not here relevant.' So the prohibition was not even rooted in scripture. It was based entirely on what Haley thought the public would stand for.

The two most conspicuous public opponents of the match were Eden and the archbishop. Eden by now had become prime minister by the skin of his trousers. A notable seducer of upper-class married women, he had already barely escaped being cited as co-respondent by his nephew Lord Warwick. In June 1950 his wife, Beatrice, agreed to be cited as the guilty party in their divorce, on the grounds that they had been separated for more than three years. By now he was having an affair with Dorothy Beatty. Her husband, son of the quasi-victor of Jutland, hoped to blackmail Eden into securing him a post in the shadow cabinet. Eden couldn't or wouldn't oblige. So Beatty put the detectives on him. Eden fled to Churchill's house at 28 Hyde Park Gate, where Churchill set up a secret HQ for him, while an officer in the Coldstream, who happened also to be in love with Dorothy, agreed to sit in Eden's house for as long as it took the detectives to identify him as the adulterous party. The obliging guardee was duly cited in the divorce proceedings, and Eden was able to become prime minister. Phew! But what a crew! Anyone who thinks Eden's deceit at Suez was out of character needs to think again.

As for the archbishop, he managed to radiate adamantine certainty. In fact the Church's position on divorce and remarriage was under extreme pressure. The Church of England had landed itself with the sternest prohibitions of any church, having shunned the Catholic let-out of annulment at a price. But what scriptural authority could these rules claim? Yes, Jesus had said that 'those whom God hath joined together, let no man put asunder.' But what about those who had sundered? How was the Church to apply its message of compassion to them?

Fisher himself admitted that Jesus had left no instructions. He had left the Church free to find its way, in reliance on his Holy Spirit. Fisher did not wish to shelter behind an unyielding rigorism. Second marriages could be spiritually blessed. In the past, the Church had made exceptions to its rules, but it could no longer afford to do so. Since 1857, the C of E had been pushed in the direction of stricter discipline, because 'the mounting tide of divorce was threatening to overthrow the whole Christian conception of marriage.' So the stricter standards were new. They didn't derive from the teachings of Jesus. They were a last-ditch attempt to hold the line. The royal family was to be deployed as an instrument of social control. And in fact Fisher succeeded in pushing through Convocation two years later an act which sought to deprive priests of their old discretion to marry divorcees.

As it happens, Princess Margaret was extremely devout all her life (without her piety having much visible impact on her conduct). Every time she flew off to the West Indies, she would first go down to the Queen's Chapel of the Savoy to receive Communion from Eric Abbott, the former dean of Westminster. On her deathbed, Archbishop Carey came to give her Communion and left her a bottle of olive oil which his wife Eileen had brought back from the Holy Land. Margaret was thrilled.

All the harsher then that she should have been a victim of such strong-armed humbug by the combined forces of Church and State. But an even worse fate was in store for her. Anthony Armstrong-Jones was already well known as a society photographer. He had been to Eton and Cambridge (he had coxed the winning Cambridge eight in the Boat Race). But he was still regarded as a common snapper. Colin Tennant, a founder member of the Princess Margaret Set, had relegated him to the servants' entrance at his wedding. When Armstrong-Jones tried to introduce himself to the fearsome Betty Kenward, the pseudonymous author of 'Jennifer's Diary' in *Queen* magazine, she snapped: 'Don't you dare address me, I don't talk to my photographers.' When she heard that Armstrong-Jones was to marry the princess, she spent the afternoon kicking the wastepaper basket. Her fury was equalled by that of Cecil Beaton, who moaned in his diary that Armstrong-Jones was 'not even a good photographer'.

Why did she marry him? The reason usually given is that she was outraged when Townsend wrote to tell her that he was engaged to be married to a young Belgian girl, breaking their (not very realistic) pact that neither would ever marry anyone else. Three weeks after their wedding, Camilla Fry, the wife of Armstrong-Jones's old friend, gave birth to a daughter, the first of his irregular offspring scattered around the country during and after his marriage to Margaret. Lord Snowdon, as he now became ('In I go Jones, out I come Snowdon'), was as compulsively unfaithful as he became compulsively unpleasant to his wife. He left vicious notes for her around the house, listing 'Twenty-four reasons why I hate you' or saying: 'You look like a Jewish manicurist.' Brown compares his behaviour in the later stages of their marriage to that of Jack Manningham, the villain in Patrick Hamilton's play

Gaslight, who sets out by a series of fiendish tricks to convince his wife that she is mad. Snowdon did actually persuade the princess to visit a psychiatrist.

She was in fact perfectly capable of looking after her own interests. She secretly briefed Nigel Dempster to settle old scores, which didn't stop her being indignant when Diana told all to Andrew Morton. During her first holiday on Mustique, Colin Tennant, who had just bought the island, asked whether as a wedding present she would like a piece of jewellery or a piece of land. She responded without hesitation: 'a piece of land'. Thinking the plot he gave her inadequate, she pulled up the boundary stakes and replanted them further out. While her back was turned, Tennant silently put the stakes back in their original holes. This to and fro went on until the princess had secured a full ten acres. Snowdon hated Tennant so much that he only visited Mustique once. He may have had a point. The princess herself described her first day on the island: 'We sat in the brush and whacked mosquitoes.' The clue is in the name.

Nor did she always receive a warmer welcome within her own family. The queen never ceased to be fond of her and, later, sorry for her, but she was busy being queen. In the Townsend crisis, the queen mother offered her little or no help. The queen's secretary Martin Charteris thought that 'she was not a mother to her child. When the princess attempted to broach the subject, her mother grew upset, and refused to discuss it.' The queen mother's dislike of unpleasantness was legendary. She refused to visit her most loyal courtiers when they were dying. One old lady in waiting is said to have actually died at Clarence House, just before one of the queen mother's famous lunches under the cedar tree in the garden. Her body was shunted into a side room and HM was not informed until the lunch was over, so as not to spoil the fun. When they were both invalids, Princess Margaret was more than once spotted pinching her mother's wheelchair.

At the end of the book, only the hardest heart would repress a twitch of sympathy. To live on the receiving end of so much gush and so much abuse, to be simultaneously spoilt rotten and hopelessly infantilised, how well would any of us stand up to it? So many functions to go to, so much dysfunction to come back to. When Princess Margaret made a guest appearance at the Borsetshire fashion show in an episode of *The Archers*, the producer said after the run-through: 'That's very good, ma'am, but do you think you could sound as if you were enjoying yourself a little more?'

'Well, I wouldn't be, would I?' the princess replied.

It was a backhanded mercy that she did not live to hear the bells ringing to celebrate the engagement of Prince Harry to a divorced American actor of mixed race. Wallis Simpson, too, must be turning in her unquiet grave.

4 January 2018

Jenny Diski's final book, *In Gratitude*, was based on the pieces she wrote for the LRB in the last two years of her life.

William Empson was one of the most influential and idiosyncratic literary critics of the 20th century. He was knighted 25 years after writing a masque for the queen.

Paul Foot, a renowned campaigning and investigative journalist, wrote 60 pieces for the LRB between 1984 and 2004.

Thomas Jones edits the LRB blog from Orvieto. *Game Theory*, a novel, will be published by John Murray.

Hilary Mantel is writing the final novel in her trilogy about Thomas Cromwell. 'Royal Bodies' was delivered as an LRB Winter Lecture in 2013.

Ferdinand Mount's latest book is *English Voices: Lives, Landscapes, Laments 1985-2016*, a collection of essays.

Caroline Murphy lives in London.

Tom Nairn's books include *The Enchanted Glass: Britain and Its Monarchy* and *The Break-Up of Britain*.

Glen Newey, who died suddenly last year, was a professor of practical philosophy at the University of Leiden, and the LRB blog's most prolific contributor.

Bee Wilson is working on a book to be called *The Way We Eat Now*.

About the *London Review of Books*

The *London Review of Books* is Europe's leading magazine of culture and ideas. Published twice a month, it provides a space for some of the world's best writers to explore a wide variety of subjects in exhilarating detail – from art and politics to science and technology via history and philosophy. In the age of the long read, the LRB remains the pre-eminent exponent of the intellectual essay, admired around the world for its fearlessness, its range and its elegance.

As well as book reviews and reportage, each issue also contains poems, reviews of exhibitions and movies, 'short cuts', letters and a diary, and is available in print, online, and offline via our app. Subscribers enjoy unlimited access to every piece we've published since 1979, the year the magazine was founded, in our digital archive. It contains all of the articles in this volume, and many more that might have made the cut. Our website (lrb.co.uk) also features a regular blog, podcasts and short documentaries, plus video highlights from our events programme on both sides of the Atlantic, and at the London Review Bookshop.

A reader recently described the LRB as 'the best thing about being a human'. Make it the highlight of your fortnight, too, by taking out a subscription: www.lrb.me/collections